Footsteps of Faith

New Testament, Volume 3

Revised Edition

You Are God's Building

by

Bernice Claire Jordan

BCM International, Inc.

201 Granite Run Drive, Suite 260, Lancaster, PA 17601
70 Melvin Avenue, Hamilton, Ontario L8H 2J5 Canada
P.O. Box 688, Weston-super-Mare, N. Somerset BS23 9PP England

Footsteps of Faith is BCM's primary Bible teaching curriculum for children's Bible Clubs. This unique series has been revised for teaching God's Word in other settings, such as Sunday school, children's church, Christian school and home schooling.

Revision Committee

Revised by Pamela Rowntree & Patricia Black
Edited by Donna Culver
David and Lois Haas
Richard Winters

Cover design & book layout:
Bert VandenBos
Fran Lines

Original title: *ACTS Volume 1*

Copyright © 1999, 2020
BCM International, Inc. All rights reserved.

ISBN 978-0-86508-213-7

CONTENTS

Course Overview iv
Introduction v
    Understand Your Children vi
    Prepare Yourself to Be God's Channel vii
    Prepare Your Lesson viii
    Prepare Your Visuals ix
    Manage Your Class Effectively ix
    Lead Your Children to Christ x
    Keep in Touch xi
    Important Information xii
Lesson 1   Jesus Returns to Heaven 1
Lesson 2   The Holy Spirit Comes to Stay 10
Lesson 3   Peter & John Heal a Man 18
Lesson 4   Ananias & Sapphira Lie to God 26
Lesson 5   The Apostles Are Put in Prison 34
Lesson 6   Stephen Dies for Jesus' Sake 42
Lesson 7   Philip Obeys the Word of God 51
Lesson 8   Saul Becomes a New Man 59
Lesson 9   Dorcas Is Raised from the Dead 68
Lesson 10 Peter Tells Cornelius the Gospel 75
Lesson 11 An Angel Frees Peter from Prison 85
Lesson 12 The First Missionaries Are Sent
                Barnabas & Saul Go to Cyprus *(Part 1)* 94
                Paul & Barnabas Go to Galatia *(Part 2)* 103
Lesson 13 Paul Is Stoned for Preaching 110
Lesson 14 Paul Takes the Gospel to Europe
                Lydia Becomes a Believer *(Part 1)* 120
                The Philippian Jailer Believes *(Part 2)* 129
Resource Section 137
Teaching Materials and Supplies 148

You Are God's Building
Course Overview

No.	Title	Theme	Scripture	Verse
1	Jesus Returns to Heaven	Christ—Foundation	Acts 1:1-12	Acts 1:11
2	The Holy Spirit Comes to Stay	Holy Spirit—Power	Acts 1:12–2:47	Acts 1:8
3	Peter & John Heal a Man	Salvation	Acts 3:1–4:31	Acts 4:12
4	Ananias & Sapphira Lie to God	Holy Living	Acts 5:1-13	Pro. 12:22
5	The Apostles Are Put in Prison	Obedience	Acts 5:12-42	Acts 5:29
6	Stephen Dies for Jesus' Sake	Joy	Acts 6:1-8:2	Matt. 5:11
7	Philip Obeys the Word of God	God's Word	Acts 8:1-8, 26-39	Luke 11:28
8	Saul Becomes a New Man	New Life	Acts 9:1-22	2 Cor. 5:17
9	Dorcas Is Raised from the Dead	Love	Acts 9:32-42	1 Pet. 1:22
10	Peter Tells Cornelius the Gospel	Accepting Others	Acts 9:43–10:48	Rom. 3:22, 23
11	An Angel Frees Peter from Prison	Prayer	Acts 12:1-24	1 Pet. 3:12
12-1	Barnabas & Saul Go to Cyprus	Witnessing	Acts 11:19-26; 12:25–13:12	John 3:17
12-2	Paul & Barnabas Go to Galatia	Witnessing	Acts 13:13-52	John 3:17
13	Paul Is Stoned for Preaching	Faithfulness	Acts 14:1-28	John 14:6
14-1	Lydia Becomes a Believer	Courage	Acts 15:35–16:15	Rom. 1:16
14-2	The Philippian Jailer Believes	Courage	Acts 16:16-34	Rom. 1:16

INTRODUCTION

Footsteps of Faith is an eight-volume Bible teaching curriculum that covers the Bible in basically chronological order. Its overall aim is to help children respond to the love of God in Christ and learn to walk in the footsteps of faith and obedience.

Each volume is complete in itself and centers around a theme that is carried through every lesson in that volume to provide for consistent learning as well as continual review and application of the Bible truth.

The course is non-graded and undated, written for teaching children ages 6-12, but adaptable to different age groups and many teaching situations. It has been used effectively in Bible Clubs, children's church programs, vacation Bible schools, and Sunday school classes, as well as in Christian schools and home school classes.

The series
- shows God at work in the world. The Old Testament points ahead to Christ's coming, revealing man's fall into sin, God's promise of a Savior and his program for accomplishing this. The New Testament records the actual fulfillment of God's program in the birth of Christ, his life and death and resurrection, the birth of the Church, the establishing of a missionary program, and the yet-to-be-fulfilled promise of Christ's return!
- teaches Bible doctrine and history along with the principles of Christian living.
- emphasizes Scripture memorization and provides Bible Study Helps, which are coordinated with the lessons and may be used as work sheets or take-home devotionals.
- is both evangelistic and Christian-growth oriented, clearly presenting the plan of salvation and emphasizing practical Christian living.

The lessons
- emphasize specific Bible truths.
- include practical, hands-on application of those truths for both Christian and non-Christian children.
- are structured with a teaching aim designed to help the teacher present the Bible truth and encourage the children to relate and apply that truth to their daily lives.

A unique review system
- is built into each volume and visualizes the main theme of that course and the complementary lesson themes.
- relates the lessons logically to each other and to the central theme of the course.
- provides a framework for remembering biblical truth so that the children can apply it in their daily lives.
- enables the teacher to review and reinforce previous lessons and memory verses quickly, regularly and in an interesting way.
- stimulates the children to *see, hear, verbalize* and *do*, thus involving them in the learning process.

Correlated visual aids enhance learning

- The Visual CD contains the following PowerPoint presentation for two tracks (KJV and NIV): the Review Chart, the Memory Verses, and the Bible Lessons. The PowerPoint presentation can be displayed on a computer screen or with a video projector. The CD is suitable for all PCs capable of running PowerPoint 97 or higher. A copy of PowerPoint 97 player is included with the CD. The disk contains a set of files in Adobe Acrobat format for use in printing full-colored flashcards. A copy of Adobe Acrobat is also included in the disk.
- *The resource CD* contains the following, all of which can be downloaded and printed:
  - *Creative Idea Menus* provide a wealth of ideas to reinforce and extend learning in programs and learning centers.
  - *Visualized Memory Verses* (available in both KJV and NIV) furnishes visual pieces for teaching every memory verse in the course.
  - *Student Memory Verse Tokens and Holders* (adapted from the Review Chart and available in both KJV and NIV) are colorful take-home review aids that encourage children to memorize the verses and help to build links from week to week.
  - *Student Bible Study Helps* are take-home devotional guides that include daily Bible reading portions, questions to answer, and a weekly activity.
- Full-color *Felt Visuals*
  - The *Figures* focus attention and encourage children to visualize scenes as you tell the Bible story.
  - The *Review Chart* provides a structured system for introducing and reviewing lessons.
  - The *Felt Backgrounds* provide a scenic backdrop for the figures and can be used as an alternative to PowerPoint or flashcard visuals on the Visual CD.

You Are God's Building,

New Testament, Volume 3 of the *Footsteps of Faith* series covers Acts, chapters 1-16. It emphasizes Christ's return to heaven, the Holy Spirit's coming to indwell believers, the birth of the Church, the Body of Christ on earth, and the spread of the gospel to the Gentiles. The course aim is three-fold: 1) to lead children to receive Jesus Christ as Savior and thus make him the foundation of their lives; 2) to teach them to recognize the presence and working of God the Holy Spirit within them as believers and to appropriate his power to live godly lives; and

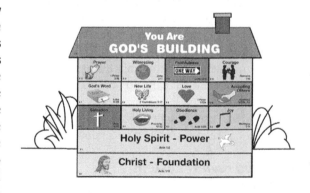

3) to communicate God's plan to build his Church on earth, including all people who will come to Christ for salvation.

Each lesson's theme is illustrated through the Bible lesson content and reflects the overall theme of building into the believer's life those truths and characteristics that will make him more Christ-like and bring honor and glory to God. The course clearly presents the plan of salvation and emphasizes practical teaching that shows children how to integrate the truths they are learning into their daily lives.

The Review Chart *You Are God's Building* is a building with building-block shaped symbols on which are printed the lesson themes and corresponding memory verse references. Whether using the Review Chart on a computer or on the felt board you will be able to take advantage of its flexibility to introduce and review Bible facts and truths as well as Bible memory verses.

Understand Your Children

Children, influenced by fast changing technology,
- access the world through computers and the internet.
- are used to a fast-paced, "instant everything" society.
- are bright, eager to learn, and well informed.
- receive much of their information in "sound bytes" (capsulized reports).
- are accustomed to seeing most problems solved within a 30- or 60-minute time slot in a television schedule; consequently, have short attention spans.
- expect great variety in all they see and hear.
- can be impatient with sitting still, being quiet or waiting.

Children, growing up in an unstable, immoral, and pluralistic world, are sometimes
- feeling a deep need for someone to love them, to care about them, to give them a reason to hope.
- being exposed by the media to too much too early.
- being conditioned to accept materialism, deteriorating moral standards, and a secular worldview as the norm.
- being assaulted by violence in the media and in their homes and neighborhoods.
- being traumatized by broken homes, tragedies, or incurable diseases.
- being left to solve problems on their own.
- being bombarded with moral and belief systems that contradict the Word of God.
- lacking a biblical world view to help them sift conflicting information.

Children learn in many different ways.
- Some learn best by *seeing* what they're learning.
- Others learn best by *talking* about it.
- Still others learn best by *moving* or *doing*—being actively involved or making things.
- Some process information globally—by seeing "the big picture."
- Others are analytic thinkers and want all the details.

Remember these things when preparing to teach. Try a variety of the teaching methods and options suggested in the text, even if they do not all appeal to you. They will help you incorporate variety in methods and visuals and capsulize important points in "sound bytes" the children can see and hear over and over. You will soon know which are most effective with your class members.

What a privilege—and what a sobering responsibility—to take to them the wonderful news that God loves them, that he has provided salvation for them and that he has a plan for their lives! There is hope in him!

For *GOD never changes*! His truth is timeless! The experiences of the Apostles and the early Church, of Stephen and Philip, Peter and Cornelius, Paul and Barnabas, Dorcas and Lydia—and other men and women of faith—speak to us truths that are relevant for today. God's eternal Word is a guidebook for living a life that pleases God in any age. Knowing him and walking in the footsteps of faith and obedience provide security and stability in an uncertain world.

Therefore, it is essential to take time to get to know your students and understand their needs, so that you can demonstrate Christ's love to them and lead them to security in him in the midst of their insecure world.

Prepare Yourself to Be God's Channel

You, the teacher, are the living link between God's truth and the children in your class. You channel Christ's love to them. You teach them God's Word so that they may understand his truth and receive Christ as Savior, then follow him in loving obedience. You model how to practice in daily life the truth they are learning. And you are their guide to discovering truth for themselves and attaining their greatest potential for serving God.

- Submit yourself to God that you may be a Spirit-empowered teacher.
- Expect God to speak to you personally as you study your lesson each week, then to guide you as you prepare to teach.
- Realize that you are a tool in God's hands. As you depend on him, he will work through you and in the hearts of the children to draw them to himself.
- Enjoy your class! Be enthusiastic; enter into activities with the children so they see you not only as teacher but as a friend.
- Encourage the children to bring their Bibles, and plan ways for them to use them every week. Teach them how to find passages in Scripture. Frequently have them follow along in their Bibles as you teach the lesson. As you instruct boys and girls to love and respect God's Word, show them how to use it correctly and inspire them to obey it, you give them an invaluable gift that will go with them throughout life. (If some don't have Bibles, look for a place to get them inexpensively—a Bible society or an organization that distributes free ones.)
- REVIEW, REVIEW, REVIEW! Without reviewing the lessons, the children will probably forget to apply many essential Bible truths you are teaching them.
- Avoid using many questions that can be answered with a simple yes or no.
- Use the questions suggested in the lesson, or others you devise yourself, to involve the children in the learning process and find out what they have or have not learned. Then you will have the opportunity to correct faulty understanding, and they will learn more because they are thinking and interacting.
- Avoid calling on students who find it difficult or embarrassing to read aloud or answer questions publicly. Find other ways to involve them until they feel safe enough to interact.

Remember that your effectiveness in class often depends upon the relationship that you have established with students outside of class.

- Find ways to spend time with students, such as attending some of their school or neighborhood activities and visiting at least some of their homes.
- Learn their names and show a real interest in them.
- Listen when they talk about their families, their friends, and their struggles. Listening shows the child that you care and helps you learn how to apply Scripture effectively.
- Notice individual's strengths and affirm them regularly.
- Compliment those you see practicing what they're learning.
- Seek to discern the spiritual progress of individual students and help them to grow in Christlikeness.
- Don't be afraid to be explicit when dealing with the issues that surround them. They are exposed to life experiences and life styles far beyond what they should be. They need to know what God has to say and how to live for him in the midst of their life situations. Ask God to guide you and make you sensitive to their needs and his direction.
- Pray for them.
- Make the brief time they spend with you each week a happy time, a safe place—a refuge.

Prepare Your Lesson

Pray that God will speak to you through the Scripture passage, then guide you as you prepare to teach.

- Follow the plan in the teacher's text or use it as a pattern to write your own. A lesson plan will keep you on track, by helping you use your time wisely and accomplish the purpose God lays on your heart for the lesson.
- Study the Scripture passage thoroughly, making notes of points that seem important to you. Look for answers to six important questions: *Who* was involved? *What* was happening? *Where* were they? *When* did it happen? *How* did it happen? *Why* did it happen? or *Why* did he say that?
- Make simple outline notes to use as a guide when teaching. Put them in your Bible so that the children will see you teaching from God's Word, not the teacher's text.
- Read the printed lesson, thinking it through with your children in mind. Each part of the lesson has a specific purpose.

    The **Aim** is the statement of what you want to accomplish—with God's help—as you present the lesson.

    The **Introduction** is a plan for getting the students' attention and directing their thinking in preparation for the Bible story.

    The **Bible Content** is the Bible story and the Bible truth it illustrates and reinforces.

    The **Conclusion** is a plan for completing the lesson by showing the children how to apply the Bible truth and providing a way for them to respond to it in daily life.

Prepare Your Visuals

When using the Visual CD:

- Become familiar with how the visual CD is programmed. Learn how to access the Review Chart and to work with the memory verse. Become familiar with accessing the lesson and coordinating the PowerPoint visuals with the teacher's text.
- To show the PowerPoint slides on a screen, connect your computer to a video projector.
- Practice as many times as necessary to become proficient in using the PowerPoint visuals with the lesson.
- To prepare flashcards to visualize the lesson, click on the print icon on the title page of the PowerPoint lesson. Print the scenes on the size paper you want and laminate them to increase their continued use.

When using the Felt Visuals:

- Sort out the figures you will need and stack them in the order you will use them.
- Put the Review Chart and the backgrounds on the felt storyboard in the order they will be used, with the last background on the bottom. Secure them to the top of the board with large binder clips.
- Use the sketches in the lesson as guides for placing figures on scenes. Practice placing the figures as you stand at the side of the board. Check from the front to see if they are straight and in their proper places. Sometimes it is helpful to put some of the figures on the backgrounds ahead of time so that you just add the main figure(s) while telling the story.
- Practice telling the story aloud as you put the figures in place until you can do it comfortably and without interruption.
- When you teach, be careful to always work from the side of your board so you don't block a student's view. Maintain eye contact with the children and don't turn your back on them.

Manage Your Class Effectively

A well-managed classroom honors God by creating an atmosphere for learning, providing a secure refuge for students, making learning enjoyable, and preventing many behavior and discipline problems. A well-managed classroom requires three elements.

A prepared teacher
- yielded to God in mind, heart, and spirit
- ready with both lesson and program
- knowing each student's name, characteristics, needs, and interests
- praying for each student
- planning behavioral goals for the children
- arriving early to prepare the room before the children arrive

A prepared environment
- visuals and equipment set up and in working order
- appropriate seating arranged so all can see and hear
- comfortable temperature and adequate lighting
- minimal distractions (e.g., clutter, noise, activities)

Prepared students
- knowing class rules: for example, where to put their coats, where to say their verses, how to answer or ask questions, enter and leave class, or take bathroom breaks
- aware that you expect them to obey class rules, that you appreciate good behavior and will praise them for it, and that there will be consequences for inappropriate behavior

The ultimate purpose of managing your class well is to create an environment in which God the Holy Spirit is able to work through the Word of God to bring about change in the children's lives.

Lead Your Children to Christ

Leading children to receive Jesus Christ as their Savior is a glorious privilege and an awesome responsibility. It is our deep conviction that to adequately carry out this responsibility the teacher must do four things:
- Present salvation truth frequently.
- Give students opportunities to respond to the truth.
- Speak privately with those who respond.
- Follow up on those who make a profession of faith.

In class
- *Present salvation truth.*
  "God is holy. We are sinners, deserving punishment. We must believe the Lord Jesus Christ died for us and receive him as our personal Savior."
  Use the salvation ABCs:
  - ADMIT I am a sinner: I've done wrong things, displeased God (Romans 3:23).
  - BELIEVE that Jesus Christ is God, that he died on the cross for me, and that he rose again (Romans 5:8).
  - CHOOSE to receive Christ as Savior and Lord (Romans 10:9).
- *Invite the children to respond.*
  "Perhaps you have never received Christ as your Savior and would like to do that today. If so, I'd like to talk with you after class and show you how."

After class

Talk individually with those who respond, being careful to have the door open and a helper nearby.
- Find out if they understand why they came.
  - "Is there a special reason you came to talk to me?"
  - "Have you ever received Jesus as your Savior before?"
- *Review basic facts about Christ.*
  - Who Jesus is (both God and man) John 3:16; 1 John 5:20
  - What Jesus did (died on the cross to take the punishment for our sins; rose again to be our living Savior) 1 Corinthians 15:3, 4
  - Why they need Jesus ("You are a sinner deserving punishment for your sins. Jesus can make you right with God and give you eternal life in heaven"). Romans 3:10; 6:23
- *Review the ABCs of salvation listed above.*
  - Say, "Jesus wants to be your Savior right now. Will you receive him?" John 1:12
  - If they say yes, ask them to pray aloud. Let them use their own words, but guide them if necessary ("I admit I am a sinner, I'm sorry for my sins and want to be free from them. I believe you died for me, and I receive you as my living Savior.")
  - Be sure they base their salvation on God's Word, not on their feelings! Show them Scriptures (Romans 10:9; John 1:12; 1 John 5:11-13) that indicate salvation is by faith, believing what God says.
- *Follow up.*
  Give them the tract entitled *"A Child of God,"* as a reminder of what they have done. Read through it with them. Then use it as a guide for Christian growth in the weeks ahead.

Keep in Touch

Use Mailbox Bible Club correspondence lessons to keep in touch after the series is finished. When the children return their completed lessons (either by mail or in person) to be checked and to receive the next lesson, you have an excellent opportunity to answer questions and provide continuing guided help for their walk with the Lord. *(See the Teaching Materials & Supplies list on page 148 for information on ordering materials and obtaining a lesson sample.)*

**Do you have suggestions or questions? Do you need help or training?
Contact us at**

BCM INTERNATIONAL, INC.
201 Granite Run Drive, Suite 260, Lancaster PA 17601
Toll-free: 1-888-226-4685; FAX: 1-717-560-9607
email: publications@bcmintl.org

70 Melvin Avenue, Hamilton, ON L8H 2J5 Canada
Phone: 1-905-549-9810; FAX: 1-905-549-7664
email: mission@bcmintl.ca

P.O. Box 688, Weston-super-Mare, N. Somerset BS23 9PP England
Phone: +(44) 7845-174853; email: office@bcm.org.uk

Important Information
About the Teaching Materials for This Course

Listed below are general visual aids you should have available before you begin teaching the course, along with instructions for preparing some teaching aids that are used in most lessons. Check the "Materials to Gather" section in each lesson for items to collect for that lesson. Choose from the Options those learning activities that are appropriate for the various learning styles in your group.

PowerPoint visuals available on the Visual CD (FN3VCD)

Use a computer or a video projector to display the Lesson, Memory Verse, and Review Chart visuals. If you do not have PowerPoint 97 or higher in your computer, install it free by following the directions on page 5 of the guidebook that comes with the Visual CD. The visuals are programmed to follow the sequence of the lesson in the text. Click on the right arrow of the computer to add or remove figures and to change sketches when the lesson text tells you to place, add, or remove the figures. You can use colored flashcards to teach the lessons by clicking on the "Print icon" on each lesson's title slide.

Visualized memory verses available on the Resource CD (FN3RCD)

Print the visuals on heavy paper and cut them out. Place each verse in a separate file folder.

Memory verse tokens & token holders available on the Resource CD

Use these as an incentive to memorize weekly Bible verses (available in KJV and NIV). Print the holders on card stock. Print the colored tokens and cut them out before class. When the students can say a verse correctly, have them paste its token on their token holders. Or, paste all tokens on the token holders; then let those who say the verse correctly put a small sticker on their token. (Prepare an extra set of tokens if you want to give a token to each child after class to practice the verse at home.) Send the token holders home at the end of the course.

Bible Study Helps available on the Resource CD

To encourage daily Bible reading, print and give out one lesson at a time to each student to take home. Have the children bring their completed sheets the next week for you to check.

Felt Figures

Cut out the figures and file them in numerical order in file folders labelled 1-10, 11-19, etc.

Felt Backgrounds

Order from BCM or use your own flannelgraph backgrounds (the *Felt Figures* will adhere to the flannel).

Patterns & Maps: Use a copier to enlarge and print the patterns and map indicated. Attach these visuals (or any chart you make) to the felt board with clips or loops of tape when indicated.

Word strips & cards: Word strips are available in the Felt Figure's packet. If you are not using the felt figures, use your computer to prepare and print word strips and cards specified for each lesson. Cut them apart and glue small pieces of double-faced flannel to the back of the strips so that they will adhere to the felt board. Or, print the words clearly on quality paper towel or construction paper strips, and use sandpaper to roughen the back of the construction paper strips.

Handouts: Use a copier to duplicate the pattern specified in Materials to Gather.

For information about ordering any of the above teaching materials see page 148.

Jesus Returns to Heaven
Theme: Christ – Foundation

Lesson 1

 BEFORE YOU BEGIN...

Children seem to be fascinated by what will happen to them in the future and wondering if they will really go to heaven someday. In an uncertain world where hope and security are often tenuous, boys and girls need to know there is someone they can trust—a secure hope for the future, a solid foundation for their lives today.

This lesson presents clearly how we can have Jesus Christ as the firm foundation of our lives. It also declares both the hope we have for heaven through trusting him as Savior and his sure promise to return to earth someday. As you prepare, allow God to reveal to your heart afresh the wonderful truth of the hope we have in Christ for now and eternity. Then trust him to communicate that truth through you so your children will understand their need and God's provision. *"Blessed is the man [or the child] who trusts in the Lord, and whose hope is the Lord"* (Jeremiah 17:7, NKJV).

☞ **AIM:**

That the children may

- Know that Jesus Christ will become the foundation of their lives and make them ready for heaven when they accept him as Savior.

- Respond by accepting Christ as Savior and thanking him for making them ready for heaven.

 SCRIPTURE: Acts 1:1-12; Matthew 28:19, 20; Luke 24:46-53

 MEMORY VERSE: Acts 1:11

This same Jesus, which is taken up from you into heaven, shall so come in like manner as ye have seen him go into heaven. (KJV)
This same Jesus, who has been taken from you into heaven, will come back in the same way you have seen him go into heaven. (NIV)

📁 MATERIALS TO GATHER

Memory verse visual for Acts 1:11 (see page xii)
Backgrounds: Review Chart, Plain Background (solid color), General Outdoor
Figures: 1R, R1, 1, 3, 3A, 3B, 3C, 3D, 3E, 4, 5, 6A, 6B, 6C, 6D, 6E, 6F, 7A, 7B, 8(2), 18, 40, 71
Token holders & memory verse tokens (see page xii) for Acts 1:11
Bible Study Helps for Lesson 1 (see page xii)
Special:
- *For Review Chart:* An architect's drawing (optional)
- *For Bible Content 1:* Word strips: MATTHEW, MARK, LUKE, JOHN
- *For Bible Content 2:* Word strips: ACTS, COMMAND, PROMISE, I AM WITH YOU ALWAYS.
- *For Summary:* Word strips PROMISE, I AM WITH YOU ALWAYS.
- *For Response Activity:* "Jesus and Me" handouts, pencils
- *For Options:* Materials for any options you choose to use
- *Note:* Follow the instructions on page xii to prepare the word strips and the "Jesus and Me" handout (pattern P-3 found on page 140).

🏠 REVIEW CHART

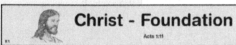

Have the Review Chart, architect's drawing, 1R and R1 ready to use when indicated.

Have you ever thought of growing up as being something like building a house? Probably not, but there are many similarities between building a house and growing up to be a person who pleases God in *every* way.

When someone wants to build a house, where does he begin? *(Encourage response.)* He needs to have a plan to show him *how* to build the house and what materials to use *(show architect's drawing)*. Then he must study and follow the plan carefully, using the proper materials, so that his house will be strong and properly built and last a long time.

As we grow up, we need a plan not only to grow strong physically, but also to become the kind of people who please God in our words, actions, and thoughts. This plan is found in God's Word, the Bible *(hold up Bible)*. God has given us instructions for "building" into our lives the things which will make us grow into strong, honest people who will love and obey him.

This picture of our Life House *(display the Review Chart with 1R in place)* reminds us that we are building our lives day by day. As we study each lesson, we will add a building block. Every block is something that God's Word—our plan—tells us we need in order to build our lives the way God wants them to be.

We will begin by placing *Christ-Foundation (place R1 on the Chart)*, the most important building block, on our Life House. What is the purpose of a building's foundation? *(Response)* It is to be a firm base on which the building is built. It is usually made of cement or cement blocks and is built into a hole which has been dug into the ground. It gives support to the building to keep it from falling down or sinking into the ground.

The foundation for our Life House is a person, the Lord Jesus Christ. The Bible tells us that God provided this Foundation, for he knew we could not do it for ourselves (1 Corinthians 3:11). He sent Jesus to the earth to be our Savior, for he knew we would need someone to save us and to give us strength to live to please him and to give us hope for the future. Today we will learn how we can have Jesus as the foundation for our life.

♥ MEMORY VERSE

Use the visual to teach Acts 1:11 as part of Bible Content 4. (I)

📖 BIBLE LESSON OUTLINE

Jesus Returns to Heaven

▪ Introduction

Preparing for Jake's visit

▪ Bible Content

1. Jesus is a very special Person.
   a. Jesus is the Son of God.
   b. Jesus was the greatest Miracle Worker.
   c. Jesus was the greatest Teacher.
   d. Jesus died on the cross.
   e. Jesus rose from the dead.
2. Jesus gives his disciples two commands and two promises.
   a. The first command and promise
   b. The second command and promise
3. Jesus returns to heaven.
4. Jesus will return to earth.
   Memory verse presentation
5. The disciples obey Jesus' command.

▪ Conclusion

Summary

Application
Making Jesus the foundation of your life

Response Activity
Accepting Jesus as Savior or thanking him for making them ready for heaven

🔺 Note (I)

If you choose to display the memory verse on the felt board, put it on a plain background throughout this volume.

▲ Option #1

Have the children read the names of these books in unison.

If time permits at this point or later in the class, help the class memorize the names of these four books in order.

And/or, have the children locate the beginning of each book in their Bibles.

And/or, conduct a Bible drill to locate each of the four books.

📖 BIBLE LESSON

■ Introduction

Preparing for Jake's visit

Billy was feeling sad and lonely. His best friend, Jake, had just moved across the country and Billy wouldn't see him again for at least a whole year! They had done everything together—had always been in the same class at school and on the same sports teams. What would he do now? Sure, he had other friends, but Jake was special.

Then a letter came from Jake. Billy couldn't believe his eyes! Jake's father was coming on a weekend business trip sometime in the next two months and had promised to bring Jake with him to visit Billy! How exciting! Billy started making plans right away.

As he reread Jake's letter, Billy realized that Jake had not said when he was coming. He just said he would call Billy a day or two before they left because his dad would not know the time until the last minute. Billy looked around his room and thought, "I better get this place cleaned up and keep it that way. Jake might call tomorrow." He didn't want to have a messy room when Jake arrived.

In today's Bible story we will learn how something very similar happened to Jesus' disciples. Jesus was their best friend and they had spent much time with him. But now things were going to change for them. Let's find out what the change was and how the disciples reacted.

■ Bible Content

1. Jesus is a very special person.

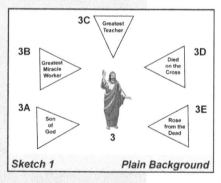

Sketch 1   Plain Background

(Jesus 3, triangles 3A, 3B, 3C, 3D, 3E; word strips MATTHEW, MARK, LUKE, JOHN)

Jesus' disciples had worked and lived with him *(place 3 on the board)* for more than three years. They loved him and had come to trust him as their Savior. We read about his life in the first four books of the New Testament of the Bible. *(Add MATTHEW, MARK, LUKE, JOHN)*. Let's read their names together. *(Do so.)* ▲#1 These books are called the Gospels. They tell us why Jesus was so special and important to his disciples. They also help us understand how special and important Jesus is to us and to the whole world! *(Remove the word strips.)* ▲#2

a. Jesus is the Son of God.

As God's Son *(add 3A)*, Jesus is both God and man. There is no one else like him. Because he is God, he is holy which means he never sinned. He never did or thought anything that was wrong.

b. Jesus was the greatest Miracle Worker.

A miracle is something wonderful that people cannot do. Jesus performed miracles *(add 3B)* to show that God's awesome power was greater than any other. Can you name some of the miracles he did? *(For example, feeding 5,000, raising Lazarus from the dead, healing the man who was blind, walking on the water)*

c. Jesus was the greatest Teacher.

Good teachers know how to get our attention. They know how to explain things so we can understand. Because he was God, Jesus was the greatest Teacher *(add 3C)*. He knew everything about everything and all about everyone and always taught the truth. Many times he taught people by using stories called parables. Can you think of a parable Jesus told? *(For example, the good Samaritan, the prodigal son, the Sower and the seed)* He used these stories to help people understand what God is like: his love, his holiness, his forgiveness.

d. Jesus died on the cross.

Jesus came to earth from heaven in order to make a way for people to come to God and be made ready to go to heaven someday. God is holy; there is no sin in him, and there is no sin in heaven. But all people, like you and I, are born as sinners. The Bible says we have sinned (Romans 3:23) and deserve to be punished for our sin (Romans 6:23). The punishment for sin is to be forever separated from God. ▲#3

But God sent Jesus to take our punishment. He gave up his life and died in our place *(add 3D)*. He was the only one who could do this, for he had no sin in him. By dying for us, he made a way for us to be forgiven for our sin. What a wonderful hope we have! Someday we will live with God forever.

e. Jesus rose from the dead.

After Jesus died on the cross, his body was buried in a grave. But then a miracle happened! He rose again three days later *(add 3E)* so that all who believed in him would be saved from the punishment for sin. Jesus was the only one who could do this, for he was God. He provided the only way that people can be forgiven for their sin and made ready to live with him in heaven some day.

This helps us understand why Jesus was so special to his disciples and why they were so thrilled because he was actually with them again, talking and eating with them just as he had before he died on the cross!

After Jesus rose from the dead, he stayed on the earth for 40 days. During that time many people saw him and talked with him. He appeared to his own disciples many times, for he knew they were confused and afraid and had many questions. One day he appeared to

---

▲ Option #2

Use teaching pictures and/or visuals from your collection to illustrate the parables, the miracles, and Jesus death and resurrection. Or, illustrate as you teach by drawing simple stick figures on chalkboard, whiteboard or newsprint. If time permits, have the children make simple drawings—either as a mural or as individual pictures—to illustrate the miracles and parables and later be hung on the wall of your classroom.

▲ Option #3

Definition word cards:
Holy = having no sin.
Sin = choosing your own way instead of God's way.

Print the word on one side of a flash card; the definition on the reverse.

Peter alone and another time, to his half-brother James (1 Corinthians 15:3, 7). Once he met and talked with more than 500 people. Jesus loved his followers and spent time with them, answering their questions and teaching them many things. He did not have much time, for he knew he must soon go back to heaven to be with God the Father.

2. Jesus gives his disciples two commands and two promises.
(Acts 1:4, 5; Matthew 28:19, 20; Mark 16:15; Luke 24:46-49)

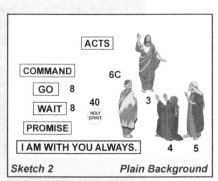
Sketch 2   Plain Background

(Word strips ACTS, COMMAND, PROMISE, I AM WITH YOU ALWAYS; Luke 1, Jesus 3, Peter 4, James 5, disciple 6C, WAIT 8, HOLY SPIRIT 40, GO 8)

Today we will begin studying the fifth book of the New Testament—a very exciting book. Let's find it. It comes right after John. What is it called? *(Response)* Yes, Acts or The Acts of the Apostles *(place ACTS on the board)*. This book was written by a doctor named Luke *(add 1)* as a letter to his friend Theophilus. It was his second book. Earlier he had written a letter to Theophilus telling about Jesus' life on earth. We call that letter the book of Luke or the Gospel according to Luke, the third book of the New Testament. God guided Luke in writing both of these books and preserved them so they would not be changed or lost *(remove 1)*.

The word *acts* means *things people do*. The word *apostles* means *sent ones* and is another name for the disciples Jesus chose to follow him *(add 3, 4, 5, 6C)* and work with him while he was here on earth. In Acts we learn how Jesus—before he went back to heaven—"sent" his disciples to tell people all over the world about him. That's why they are called apostles in the book of Acts. We also are going to learn the exciting story of their "acts" or works as they obeyed Jesus.

It begins by telling us some of the things Jesus told his disciples just before going back to heaven. He gave them two commands *(add COMMAND)* and two promises *(add PROMISE)*. The commands would answer their questions about what they were to do. The promises would comfort and encourage them after he had gone.

a. The first command and promise

Who knows what a command is? *(Response)* It is something you are told to do by a person who has authority over you. Jesus' first command to the disciples was to wait *(add 8)* in Jerusalem after he left. ▲#4

Who can tell us what a promise is? *(Response)* It is an agreement or a commitment by a person to do something. Jesus' first promise was that the Holy Spirit *(add 40)* would come to be in them and help them to be strong and to obey Jesus' next command.

▲ **Option #4**

Definition word cards:
Command = something you are told to do.
Promise = a commitment to do something.

Print the word on one side of a flash card; the definition on the reverse.

b. The second command and promise

Jesus' second command was that they were to GO *(add 8)* into all the world and preach the gospel, the Good News about Jesus, to everyone! What is the Good News about Jesus? *(Response)* Yes, it is that Jesus died and rose again in order to take the punishment we deserve for our sin. He made a way by which everyone in the world could be forgiven for their sin and be sure of going to heaven someday. Preaching this wonderful message to the *whole* world must have seemed like a huge job to these men and probably very scary. The world was a *big* place to them. How would they ever be able to do it?

But then Jesus gave them a second wonderful promise. He told them that he would always be with them *"(add I AM WITH YOU ALWAYS)*. They could not understand how he could be with them always when he was going to go away and leave them, but his promise comforted them and gave them hope. They trusted him even when they did not understand what he was talking about.

3. Jesus returns to heaven.
(Mark 16:19; Luke 24:50-53;
Acts 1:6-9; 2:33; Hebrews 1:3)

(Jesus 3, disciples 4, 5, 6B, 6C, 6D, 6E, 6F)
One day when they were talking about these things, they came to a place called the Mount of Olives *(place all the figures on the board)*. Jesus finished telling them all he wanted them to do after he was gone (Acts 1:8). Then, as he lifted up his hands to bless them, he was taken up from them into heaven and a cloud hid him from their sight. *(Remove 3 by slowly moving it up into the sky and off the board.)*

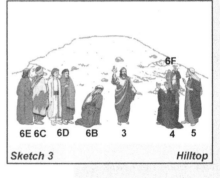

Sketch 3 — Hilltop

The Bible doesn't tell us much about what happened when Jesus returned to heaven, but it does say that he sat down at the right hand of God, the Father, which is the highest place of honor (Acts 2:33; Hebrews 1:3). He had finished his work on earth. What a celebration there must have been in heaven that day! *(Leave all the figures on the board.)*

4. Jesus will return to earth.
(Acts 1:10, 11; Matthew 24:42-44;
1 Thessalonians 4:14-18; Titus 2:11-13)
Memory verse presentation

(Men 7A, 7B)
How do you think the disciples felt as they watched Jesus going up into heaven? *(Response)* Were they surprised? Did they find it hard to believe what they were seeing? Do you think they felt sad or maybe even afraid?

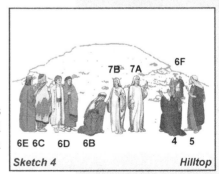

Sketch 4 — Hilltop

Suddenly two men *(add 7A, 7B)* in shining white clothing appeared in front of them and said, "Why are you standing here looking up into the sky?" Then they gave them a wonderful promise, which is our memory verse today. *(Remove all the figures.)*

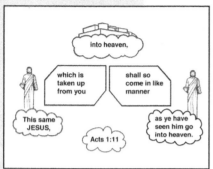

(Visual for Acts 1:11)
Display the verse; read it aloud together.
What was the promise? *(Response)* Yes, that this *same* Jesus – the very One the disciples had loved and trusted and watched go to heaven – would come back again.

How will he come? Yes, in the same way he left. How did Jesus leave them? *(Response)* Yes, in a real body, so he will come back in a real body. He went up into the clouds; he will come back in the clouds. He went away as a real, living person; he will come back as a real living person.

When will Jesus return? Does the verse tell us? No, it doesn't. The Bible says that God the Father is the only person who knows when Jesus will come back. It also tells us that when Jesus comes, he will take all those who have trusted him as Savior back to heaven to live with him forever. We need to be ready, for he could come back at any time. What a wonderful hope we have! *(Work on memorizing the verse.)* ▲#5

▲ Option #5

Memorizing the verse: Use the following actions to help the children learn the verse. Go over the verse several times using the visual as well as the actions. Then have them try to say the verse without the visual.

"This same Jesus" *Extend both arms forward.*

"which is taken up from you into heaven" *Swing both arms upward.*

"shall so come in like manner" *Bring both arms downward.*

"as ye have seen him go into heaven." *Extend both arms upward.*

5. The disciples obey Jesus' command.
   (Acts 1:12-14; Luke 24:52, 53)

How do you think the disciples felt now? *(Response)* Yes, they must have been filled with joy and hope for they knew that they could trust Jesus to keep his promise. They would see him again for they had made him the foundation of their lives by trusting in him as Savior. As they walked back toward Jerusalem, they had a lot to think and talk about. Jesus had told them what they were to do and now they had to obey.

■ Conclusion

Summary

(Jesus 3, disciples 4, 5, Holy Spirit 40; word strips PROMISE, I AM WITH YOU ALWAYS.)
What two promises did Jesus *(place 3 and PROMISE on the board)* give his disciples? *(Add 4, 5; allow for response throughout.)* The Holy Spirit *(add 40)* would come to be in them and Jesus would be with them always *(add I AM WITH YOU ALWAYS.)*

What promise did the angels give to the disciples? Yes, Jesus would come again! This promises gave them hope that they would see him again someday!

Why were the disciples able to have hope and obey Jesus even when they didn't understand? They were ready for his return for they had made him the foundation of their lives. Having the Lord Jesus as the foundation for our Life House will give us hope, too, because it will make us ready to live in heaven with him someday. And just as the foundation of a house helps it to stand strong and not fall down, the Lord Jesus will help us build strong lives that please God.

Application ▲#6

(Girl 18, boy 71)
How can we *(add 18, 71)* make Jesus the foundation for our lives?
We must:
- Admit we need his forgiveness because we're sinners.
- Believe Jesus died on the cross to take our punishment and then rose again from the dead.
- Choose to receive Christ as our Savior and Lord.

When we do this:
- God forgives our sin and makes us ready to meet Jesus.
- Jesus becomes the foundation for our lives. We can then begin to "build" our lives day by day on Jesus, using the Word of God as our plan and guide.

Have you made Jesus the Foundation of your life? Would you be ready to meet him if he should return today? Let's make sure now.

Response Activity

Distribute the **"Jesus and Me" handouts** and pencils. Read through the statements aloud, giving the children time to think about each one. Have them place a check mark beside any of the statements that are true for them. (2)

Close in prayer, inviting those who have already trusted Jesus as Savior to thank him for their salvation and for his promise that he is coming again. Encourage the children to share their responses with you after class. Be prepared to help any who want to trust Christ as Savior or those who may have questions.

✍ TAKE HOME ITEMS

Distribute **memory verse tokens for Acts 1:11** and **Bible Study Helps for Lesson 1**. Challenge the children to review the verse so that they can say it next week. Encourage them to take time each day to read the assigned Scripture verses in the Bible Study Helps, answer the questions and pray, asking God to help them remember and obey what they have read. Explain that it is more effective to do the reading one day at a time than to do it all at once. Next week ask if they did it and if they have any questions about it. (3)

▲ Option #6

Print these points on newsprint or chalkboard to use as a visual. Or print each point on a flash card for a child to hold as you teach.

Our part:
- Admit
- Believe
- Choose

God's part:
- Forgives us
- Makes Jesus our foundation.

Note (2)

Be sensitive to each student's response to the salvation message. Since this may be the first exposure to this truth for many children, it is important not to pressure them for a decision. Many need more information and/or time; thus the number of response choices given in the handout. The responses you receive from the children should help you in planning your future lessons and applications.

Note (3)

Regular Bible reading is necessary to the spiritual health and growth of believers. Give the Bible Study Helps to your children and encourage them week by week to develop this important habit. As an incentive, have them bring the completed sheet back next week to receive a sticker.

To obtain inexpensive Bibles, contact:
American Bible Society
http://americanbible.org

The Holy Spirit Comes to Stay
Theme: Holy Spirit – Power

Lesson 2

 BEFORE YOU BEGIN...

Today we are constantly bombarded with the idea that we can do anything we set our minds to, for the power to do it comes from somewhere within us. Of course, it is true that we all are given minds to think and abilities to accomplish tasks. But that we can accomplish all things and need no other source of power is *not* true. However, children are regularly fed this message through the media. What happens when they discover that they do not have the power or strength they need within themselves?

What does the Bible say? As you prepare to teach this lesson, you will realize again that God's plan for the believer's power is the Holy Spirit living within us. Jesus' disciples were fearful and powerless to be his witnesses until God the Holy Spirit came upon them at Pentecost. Help your children understand that when they accept Christ as Savior, God the Holy Spirit comes to dwell in them, that he will never leave them, and that they can then draw on his power and strength to obey God's commands, just as the disciples took courage from him to go out and share the gospel. *"His divine power has given to us all things that pertain to life and godliness" (2 Peter 1:3, NKJV).*

☞ **AIM:**

That the children may

- Know that the Holy Spirit comes to live in those who trust the Lord Jesus as Savior and gives them power to obey God.
- Respond by trusting Christ as Savior and then relying on the Holy Spirit's power to help them obey.

📖 **SCRIPTURE:** Acts 1:12-26; 2:1-47; Leviticus 23:4-16; Joel 2:28-32

♥ **MEMORY VERSE:** Acts 1:8

But ye shall receive power, after that the Holy Ghost is come upon you; and ye shall be witnesses unto me. (KJV)
But you will receive power when the Holy Spirit comes on you; and you will be my witnesses. (NIV)

📁 MATERIALS TO GATHER

Memory verse visual for Acts 1:8
Backgrounds: Review Chart, Plain Background, General Interior, City Street, River
Figures: 1R, R1, R2, 6A, 6B, 6D, 6E, 11, 12, 13, 14, 15, 16, 17, 18, 71
Token holders & memory verse tokens for Acts 1:8
Bible Study Helps for Lesson 2
Special:
- *For Memory Verse:* Word strip: TRINITY; Trinity circles
- *For Summary:* "Trinity" circles
- *For Application:* Newsprint & marker or chalkboard & chalk
- *For Response Activity:* "Trinity Circle" handouts; pencils
- *For Options:* Materials for any options you choose to use
- *Note: Follow the instructions on page xii to prepare the word strip and the "Trinity Circle" handouts (pattern P-11 on page 144). To prepare the Trinity circles, cut two circles from flannel or felt, print GOD on one circle. Divide the other circle into three equal parts (see pattern P-11 on page 144). Print God the Father on one section; God the Son on the second section; and God the Holy Spirit on the third. Cut the sections apart.*

🏠 REVIEW CHART

Display the Review Chart with 1R in place. Review the theme and memory verse from the last lesson by having the whole class say the verse together as one child places R1 on the Chart. Have R2 ready to use when indicated. Use the following questions to review Lesson 1: **(1)**

Note (1)

We have positioned the "Holy Spirit – Power" block in the foundation of the Life House because from the moment of salvation the Holy Spirit is resident within all believers to enable us to obey God and grow into mature Christians. Carefully teach your children that God expects us to be active participants with the Holy Spirit in the process of growing—of "building" our Life Houses. Emphasize that real and lasting change comes about not by self-effort, but as we cooperate with the Holy Spirit who is at work within us to make us like Christ.

Holy Spirit - Power
Acts 1:8

1. Who should be the foundation for our Life House? *(Christ or Jesus Christ)*
2. What two commands did Jesus give his disciples before going back to heaven? *(To wait and to go)*
3. How did Jesus go back to heaven? *(He went upward and disappeared into a cloud while the disciples watched.)*
4. What promise did the angels give to the disciples? *(That Jesus would come back again; have the children say Acts 1:11 together.)*
5. How can we be ready for his return? *(By trusting Jesus as Savior and obeying his Word)*

Today's building block for our Life House is *Holy Spirit – Power* (place R2 on the Chart). What do you think of when you hear the word *power? (Allow for response.)* ▲#1 Perhaps someone who has big muscles and is very strong. Or cars that can go very fast or machines that are created to do big jobs. ▲#2

▲ Option #1

Print responses to the word *power* on newsprint, chalkboard, or whiteboard. Or, provide newsprint and markers or crayons. Have the children—individually or in small groups—make drawings illustrating what power means to them.

▲ Option #2

Let the children demonstrate their strength by lifting objects of varying weights; e.g., a pencil, a stack of books or some hand weights. Be sure to do this safely.

◬ **Note (2)**

Ghost and *Spirit* have the same meaning. We generally prefer to use the word Spirit because the word ghost has been associated with the make-believe and the scary.

▲ **Option #3**

Definition word card:
Trinity = 3-in-one.

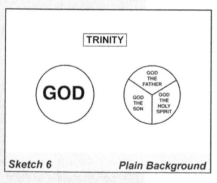

Sketch 6 — Plain Background

The power we want to talk about today means strength, too, but not the kind that can lift heavy things. It is the strength and ability God gives to us so we can do what he tells us to do, even when it is very difficult or scary. Without the Holy Spirit we would not be able to build our Life House. Our memory verse and Bible lesson will help us understand more about this wonderful power.

♥ **MEMORY VERSE**

Use the visual to teach Acts 1:8 when indicated.

Just before Jesus went back to heaven, he commanded his disciples to take the gospel, the good news about Jesus, to the whole world. That must have seemed like an impossible thing to do. But when Jesus spoke his last words to them, he told them how they would be able to obey this command. *(Display the reference and the first five visual pieces and read it aloud together. Allow for response throughout.)* ◬**(2)** According to these words, what did Jesus tell his disciples they would receive? *(Power)* Where did Jesus say this power would come from? *(The Holy Ghost/Holy Spirit)* When did Jesus say they would receive this power? *(When the Holy Ghost/Holy Spirit would come)*

Who is the Holy Spirit? We can find a clue in the name. What does the word *holy* tell us? *(He is without sin.)* Who is the only one who does not have sin? That's right—God. God is the only one who is holy and so the Holy Spirit must be God.

(Word strip TRINITY; "Trinity" circles)

The Bible teaches us that there is one true God *(place the GOD circle on the board)* who is also three persons or "three-in-one." ▲**#3** We use the word trinity *(add TRINITY)* to express this three-in-one truth about God. The names of the three persons are God the Father, God the Son (who is Jesus), and God the Holy Spirit *(add second circle [3 parts] as you say the names)*. In the Old Testament we read mostly about the work of God the Father; in the Gospels we read mostly about God the Son, the Lord Jesus; and in the book of Acts we learn very much about the work of God the Holy Spirit. They are three persons, yet one God.

Many things are made up of three parts and yet are one: for example, a *triangle* (one shape with three sides) or a *tricycle* (one cycle with three wheels). God is one God in three very real Persons. It is not easy to understand this, but we must accept it by faith. ▲**#4**

What did Jesus say the Holy Spirit's power would help them be? *(Display the remainder of the verse visual and read it aloud together.)* That's right; he would help them be witnesses for him. What is a witness? *(A person who tells something that he has seen or heard.)* The disciples had *seen* Jesus do many miracles and *heard* him teach God's truth. They had also *seen* him die and *heard* him teach after the resurrection. They were to tell what they knew about Jesus until the whole world would know about him. And God the Holy Spirit would give them the power to do it. *(Work on memorizing the verse.)* ▲#5

📖 BIBLE LESSON OUTLINE

The Holy Spirit Comes to Stay

■ Introduction
Wanting to do the right thing

■ Bible Content
1. The apostles wait for the Holy Spirit.
2. The Holy Spirit comes on the Day of Pentecost.
3. The apostles witness in the power of the Holy Spirit.
4. Peter preaches in the power of the Holy Spirit.
5. Three thousand people believe in Jesus.

■ Conclusion

Summary

Application
   Acknowledging if the Holy Spirit is living in you and thinking of a time when you need the Holy Spirit's help

Response Activity
   Trusting Christ as Savior and relying on the Holy Spirit to help you

📖 BIBLE LESSON

■ Introduction

Wanting to do the right thing

Did you ever try to be good for a whole day—not doing, saying or thinking one wrong thing? What happened? *(Allow for response throughout.)* Was it easy or hard? None of us can do it because the Bible tells us we are all sinners and need help to do the right thing.

Imagine what it would be like if you could have someone with you all day, every day, who had the power and ability to help you obey! Does it sound impossible? Well, it isn't; God the Holy Spirit does just that for us! When we trust Jesus to be our Savior, the Holy Spirit comes to live in us and give us God's power to do what we should.

Today we will learn how God the Holy Spirit began to help Jesus' disciples obey his command to be his witnesses.

▲ Option #4

Explaining the Trinity: Though we can never totally grasp the concept of God as three-in-one, try using a concrete example to increase the children's understanding.

For example:

1. A triangle. On chalkboard or newsprint, draw a triangle with three equal sides. Then erase one side (or draw an incom-plete triangle) to show how it is no longer a triangle if one side is missing. A triangle is one figure with three sides—three-in-one.

2. Ice, water and steam. Bring ice, water and an electric kettle or hot pot to class. Display water and ice in containers. Boil some water to show steam. Discuss how all are forms of one substance— H_2O or water—yet three distinct parts with their own identities.

▲ Option #5

Memorizing the verse: Have the class repeat the verse aloud each time a child takes a piece of the visual off the board and hands it to someone who is seated. After all the pieces are removed, have the class say the verse one more time. Then have those children who are holding verse pieces put them on the board in correct order.

Bible Content

1. The apostles wait for the Holy Spirit. (Acts 1:12-26)

Sketch 7 — General Interior

(Women 6A, 14, men 6B, 6D, 6E, 12, 13, Peter 11)

After Jesus went back to heaven and the angels promised he would return, the disciples—or apostles, as they were now known—walked back to Jerusalem to wait for the Holy Spirit to come. ⌂(3) *(Place all the figures on the board.)* Jesus had not told them how long they would have to wait, but they obeyed him without knowing all the details. They spent much time together in an upstairs room. Others, including some of the women who had loved the Lord Jesus, his mother Mary, and his brothers, came to meet and pray with them. His brothers had not believed in him until he was raised from the dead. Now they wanted to be with those who loved him. *(Leave all the figures on the board.)*

⌂ Note (3)

The twelve were called disciples (learners) while they lived and traveled with Jesus. In Acts they are called apostles (sent ones) because Jesus had "sent" them to witness for him.

⌂ Note (4)

Hundreds of years before this, God had told his people to celebrate in a special way on certain days in the year. They were called feast days. One of the feast days was Pentecost, a time when they celebrated the harvest of grain God had given them.

2. The Holy Spirit comes on the Day of Pentecost. (Acts 2:1-3; Leviticus 23:4-16)

Ten days after Jesus went back to heaven, God the Holy Spirit came on a special feast day called Pentecost. ⌂(4)

The word *Pentecost* means fiftieth. This feast day took place 50 days after the Feast of Firstfruits, which was the feast day when Jesus rose from the dead. ⌂(5) Since Jesus was on the earth for 40 days before going back to heaven, we know that the Holy Spirit came just ten days after Jesus left.

As Jesus' followers were praying together early on the morning of the fiftieth day, the Day of Pentecost, a sound from heaven like a very strong rushing wind (perhaps sounding something like a hurricane or a tornado) filled the whole house where they were sitting. Then they saw what looked like little fires over each of their heads, and they were all filled with the Holy Spirit.

There was no wind, but the Holy Spirit's coming from heaven sounded like wind to the believers. The fire that they saw showed that the Holy Spirit had come to live in them.

The Holy Spirit did not have a physical body of his own as God the Son had. He came to live within those who loved the Lord Jesus Christ and had believed in him as Savior.

Sketch 8 — City Street

3. The apostles witness in the power of the Holy Spirit. (Acts 2:4-13)

(Apostles 6D, 6E, Peter 15, crowd 16, 17)

The apostles *(place 6D, 6E, 15 on the board)* wanted to praise the Lord for all the wonderful things that he had done. Imagine their surprise when all sorts of foreign words began to come out of their mouths. They were speaking many different languages that they had never studied. God had given them a special gift or ability that day to speak in what the Bible calls "tongues." He wanted to get the attention of the unbelieving people who were in Jerusalem and to show them that he was beginning a new ministry called the Church.

Sure enough, people *(add 16, 17)* came running to find out about the noise and the excitement. They were really surprised to hear the apostles. They could tell by looking at them that most of them were from nearby Galilee. Because of the feast there were Jewish people there from Egypt and Arabia and many other countries. They spoke a lot of different languages in their homes, but the Bible says that every one of them heard someone using his language. How did the apostles learn to speak all these different languages? God the Holy Spirit gave them the ability to do this so all these strangers could hear about Jesus.

Because they were amazed and didn't know what to think, some people said, "They are just babbling. They must be drunk and don't know what they are saying." ◿**(6)** *(Leave all figures on the board.)*

4. Peter preaches in the power of the Holy Spirit. (Acts 2:14-39; Joel 2:28-32)

Then Peter *(move 15 to the right)* stood up before them all to preach. He was no longer ashamed or afraid to say that he knew the Lord Jesus. He was strong and brave because God the Holy Spirit was living in him and giving him power. He would have died for Jesus now.

Peter said, "These men are not drunk; it's only nine o'clock in the morning. What you've been hearing is the work of the Holy Spirit. God is keeping the promise he made hundreds of years ago when he said he would pour out his Spirit upon all people. He sent Jesus of Nazareth to do miracles so that you might believe. Instead, with the help of wicked men, you crucified him. But God raised him from the dead and he has gone back to God's right hand. Now he has sent the Holy Spirit. God wants you to know that the man you rejected and crucified is your Messiah and Savior."

As the people listened, many realized that what Peter said was true. They cried out, "What shall we do?" God the Holy Spirit was helping them to see that Peter spoke the truth. They had sinned.

Peter told them to repent, or to change their thinking about sin and who Jesus is, and to let people know they believed in him. ◿**(7)**

Then God would forgive them and give them the Holy Spirit. Peter said that God would give his Holy Spirit to everyone who trusted in Christ for salvation. He also told them they should be baptized to show that they really believed in Jesus as Savior and were willing to obey him.

◿ **Note (5)**

Firstfruits: Since most Jews in OT times raised their own crops to feed their families and animals, God wanted them to remember that a plentiful harvest was a blessing from him. The feast was celebrated three days after Passover every year. The people were forbidden to eat from their harvest until they had shown their gratitude to the Lord by bringing a bundle of grain to the priest to be presented to him and then burning a lamb, four quarts of flour, and a quart of wine on the altar. It is no coincidence that Jesus rose from the dead on Firstfruits. Paul calls Jesus "Christ, the firstfruits" (1 Cor. 15:20, 23), signifying that he is the first to rise and the guarantee that all believers who have died will be raised when Jesus returns.

◿ **Note (6)**

The amazing gift of "tongues" (saying things in a language that others can understand but that the speaker has never studied) appears at several turning points in the book of Acts. In Acts 2 the Church is inaugurated among Jews; in Acts 8 "tongues" apparently authenticate the conversion of Samaritans; in Acts 10 a similar thing happens when Gentiles are first evangelized; in Acts 19 the followers of John the Baptist speak in tongues

(continued on page 16)

5. Three thousand people believe in Jesus. (Acts 2:40-47)

Sketch 9 — 6E, 6D, 15, 17, River

(Apostles 6D, 6E, Peter 15, people 17)
Place all the figures on the board.

Many of the people who believed what Peter said trusted Jesus Christ as their Savior and were forgiven of their sins. Peter and the other apostles were kept busy all day long baptizing them and teaching them. That morning there had been about 120 followers of the Lord Jesus. By the end of the day there were 3,000 who had believed and been baptized. This was the beginning of the Church, which is the Bible name for all the people around the world who have accepted Jesus as their Savior from sin.

These new believers were so filled with the love of Jesus that they began to share what they had with everyone else. Instead of quarreling or using mean words, they helped one another.

Every day the apostles taught in the temple or in people's homes, telling the story of Jesus. The people were amazed and listened gladly to the Word of God. When they believed God's Word and received Jesus Christ as their Savior, they were saved. Every day the Lord added new believers to the Church, until it was an enormous group.

■ Conclusion

Summary

(Trinity circles; verse visual for Acts 1:8; boy 71, girl 18)
Place GOD THE FATHER and GOD THE HOLY SPIRIT of the "Trinity" circle on the board.

Where did Jesus go when he left earth? *(Allow for response throughout.)* Yes, he went back to heaven *(add GOD THE SON to the circle)*.

What promise did the Lord Jesus keep on the Day of Pentecost? *(Add the verse visual.)* Yes, he sent the Holy Spirit. Who is the Holy Spirit? Yes, he is God *(add the "Trinity" GOD circle)*. Where does the Holy Spirit live now that he has come into the world? That's right; he lives in those who have trusted the Lord Jesus as Savior from sin. *(Add 71, 18; move GOD THE HOLY SPIRIT away from the circle.)*

How did the Holy Spirit help Peter and the other apostles? Yes, he gave them power to tell about Jesus and not be afraid. How did all the new believers show that the Holy Spirit was helping them too? That's right; they shared what they had and helped one another.

(continued from page 15)

when they believe in Jesus as their Messiah.

In 1 Corinthians 14:22 Paul teaches that this unique expression of the Holy Spirit is a sign to unbelieving Jews that God is embarking upon a new dimension of his plan to reach the world—extending salvation to the Gentiles and introducing his Church.

Sketch 10 — Plain Background

There is no suggestion in these passages or elsewhere in Scripture that all who are converted to Christ and indwelt by the Holy Spirit must speak in "tongues" (1 Corinthians 12:13, 30). Nor is the ability to speak in "tongues"

(continued on page 17)

Application

(Newsprint & marker or chalkboard & chalk)

Is God the Holy Spirit living in you? We learn from the Bible that if you have trusted the Lord Jesus as your Savior, the Holy Spirit lives in you and gives you his power to obey God's Word.

Can you think of a time when you might need God the Holy Spirit to help you obey God? *(Print responses. For example, being kind to others who are not kind to us; not using swear words like some do; getting homework done on time; saying no to drugs; telling someone about the Lord Jesus).* He lives in us, so we can ask him to help us any time and any place! But we must choose to ask him and accept his power to do things that seem impossible to us.

Response Activity

As you distribute the **"Trinity Circle" handouts** and pencils, remind the children of who God is and that the Holy Spirit is God. Have them print yes or no on the circle to indicate if they have asked Jesus to be their Savior. Invite unsaved children to accept Chrsit and come talk with you after class.

Encourage the children to choose—from the list you made or from their own experience—one situation where they will need God's power to help this week and print it briefly on the back of the circle. Then give them time to pray silently, asking God for his help. Close by praying that God will help each child to trust the Holy Spirit to help them this week. Encourage them to report next week how he did it.

Tell them to put the circle where they will see it and be reminded that God the Holy Spirit lives in them if they have received Jesus as Savior and that he will help them.

TAKE HOME ITEMS

Distribute **memory verse tokens for Acts 1:8** and **Bible Study Helps for Lesson 2.**

(continued from page 16)

ever associated with a particularly exalted, holy, or mature spiritual life.

A careful study of 1 Corinthians 13:8-12 indicates that speaking in "tongues" was a temporary sign gift that gradually came into disuse by the end of the Apostolic Age.

Notice that "tongues" is not mentioned in verses 9-13 and that prophecies and knowledge would stop when perfection came, indicating that "tongues" would already be gone.

Note (7)

To repent means to change your attitude toward the things of God and your thinking about sin, God and yourself. Repentance involves changing your wrong thinking about these vital matters and accepting and acting upon what the Bible says about them.

Peter & John Heal a Man
Theme: Salvation

Lesson 3

❋ BEFORE YOU BEGIN...

In a culture that often mistreats children and destroys their sense of security and hope, your boys and girls need to know that Jesus really loves them and cares about them as individuals. They are "special" to him. They need to understand that God loves them so much that he sent his only Son Jesus to rescue them from sin's punishment by dying for them. They need to experience the sense of belonging that comes to those who are born into the family of God by trusting in the powerful name of Jesus.

The healing of the man who could not walk speaks to all these needs. Unnoticed by man, unproductive and begging for daily sustenance, this man was not forgotten by God. When Peter and John met him, he was healed by faith in the name of Jesus and went leaping into life, praising God, a testimony to God's gracious goodness and power. As you prayerfully prepare for your class, trust God to speak powerfully to your children's needs, drawing the unsaved to himself and strengthening those who have trusted Jesus as Savior with the sense of belonging to God's family. *"But as many as received Him, to them He gave the right to become children of God, even to those who believe in His name"* (John 1:12, NKJV).

☞ AIM:

That the children may

- Know that Jesus is the only one who has the power to save them from God's punishment for sin.
- Respond by trusting in the Lord Jesus for salvation and by thanking him for saving them from the punishment of sin.

📖 SCRIPTURE: Acts 3; 4:1-31

♥ MEMORY VERSE: Acts 4:12

Neither is there salvation in any other; for there is none other name under heaven given among men, whereby we must be saved. (KJV)

Salvation is found in no one else, for there is no other name under heaven given to men by which we must be saved. (NIV)

📁 MATERIALS TO GATHER

Memory verse visual for Acts 4:12
Backgrounds: Review Chart, Plain Background, Plain Interior, City Street, Courtyard, Council Room/Temple
Figures: 1R, R1-R3, 6B, 6C, 6D, 6E, 11, 13, 15, 17, 24, 25, 26, 27A, 27B, 28A, 28B, 29, 31, 32A, 32B, 33, 34, 35(5)
Token holders & memory verse tokens for Acts 4:12
Bible Study Helps for Lesson 3
Special:
- *For Memory Verse:* Newsprint & marker or chalkboard & chalk
- *For Application:* Word strip JESUS
- *For Response Activity:* "Paper Cross" handouts, pencils
- *For Options:* Materials for any options you choose to use
- *Note:* Follow the instructions on page xii to prepare word strip and "Paper cross" handouts (pattern P-12 on page 144).

🏠 REVIEW CHART

Display the Review Chart with 1R in place. Place R1 and R2 as you review the themes. Have individual children say the memory verses that accompany the themes. Have R3 ready to use when indicated. Use the following questions to review Lessons 1 and 2.

Let's see how well you have been listening each week. I will read a sentence describing some people we have learned about in our Bible lessons. See if you can tell me who each one is.

1. I wrote the book of Acts. Who am I? *(Dr. Luke)*
2. We told the disciples that Jesus would come again. Who are we? *(The angels)*
3. I preached a sermon and 3,000 people believed in Jesus. Who am I? *(Peter)*
4. I come to live in those who receive Jesus as their Savior and give them power to live for him. Who am I? *(The Holy Spirit)*

Today we will add the word *Salvation* to our Review Chart *(add R3)*. Salvation is the cornerstone of our Life House. Putting a cornerstone into place officially marks the beginning of construction on a building. Salvation is a gift God gives to those who come to him through the Lord Jesus Christ to be saved from sin. It marks the beginning of building our Life House. We will learn in our memory verse exactly what this word salvation means for each of us. ▲#1

▲ Option #1

Cornerstone: Have the children tell if they've ever seen a cornerstone: what it looked like, what date was on it and how it was different from other parts of the building. If you meet in a church or another building with a cornerstone, have the class take a short trip to see it and observe where it is placed.

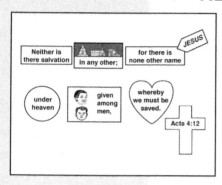

♥ MEMORY VERSE

Use newsprint & marker or chalkboard & chalk and the visual to teach Acts 4:12 when indicated.

Have you ever needed to be rescued? *(Allow for response throughout.)* Maybe from being chased by a big scary dog or being lost in a store or in the woods? Who rescued you? The person who rescued you saved you from danger or from being hurt. ▲#2

The word *Salvation* on our Life House refers to the greatest rescue you could ever have. The danger we need to be saved from is not mean dogs or a fire or being lost in a store. The Bible says we all need to be saved or rescued from the power of sin and God's punishment for sin. ▲#3

What is sin? Yes, sin is disobedience to God and his Word. Let's make a list of some of the ways we sin against God. *(Print SIN on the left side of the newsprint or chalkboard and list the children's responses under it.)* This list helps us see that anything we say, do, or even think is disobedience to God and his Word is sin. And sin must be punished by God because God is holy and just. God says that the punishment for sin is to be separated from him forever in hell.

Because God is also loving and merciful, he has made a way for us to be saved or rescued from that punishment. As we read our verse together, see if you can discover what that way is. *(Display the memory verse and read it aloud together.)* Our verse tells us that salvation is by a certain Name. Whose name do you think it is? That's right; let's say it together. *(Say JESUS together.)*. Jesus is the perfect Son of God who came to earth to take the punishment for your sins and mine. How did he do that? Yes, by dying on the cross, being punished by God the Father as though he had done every sin that has ever been done or ever will be done by people. How wonderful that after he suffered and died, he rose from the dead to live forever!

What does the verse tell us about Jesus' name? *(Print JESUS' NAME opposite SIN at the top right side of the newsprint or chalkboard and list the children's responses under it.)* We can be saved (or have salvation) by his name. His is the only name by which we can be saved. When we hear the name of Jesus, we should think of who he is and all he did in order to save us from sin's punishment. We are not saved by saying Jesus' name, but by *believing* and *accepting* what he did for us when he died on the cross and rose again from the dead. *(Work on memorizing the verse.)* ▲#4

📖 BIBLE LESSON OUTLINE

Peter & John Heal a Man

■ Introduction

The importance of a name

▲ **Option #2**

Provide newsprint and markers or crayons. Have the children (individually or as a group working on a wall mural) draw an example of being rescued and then describe the situation as they show their drawings.

▲ **Option #3**

Definition word card:
Salvation = God's gift to all who come to him through the Lord Jesus to be saved from sin.'

▲ **Option #4**

Memorizing the verse: divide the class into six groups or choose six individuals. Give each group or individual) one of the six verse parts to say aloud at the appropriate time.

Have the entire class say the verse reference. Then have each group in turn stand and say their part of the verse. Repeat several times until the class can say it without looking.

■ Bible Content

1. A baby boy is born.
2. Peter and John help the man who could not walk.
3. Peter witnesses to the crowd.
4. The Jewish leaders put Peter and John in prison.
5. The Jewish leaders threaten Peter and John.
6. The apostles pray for boldness.

■ Conclusion

Summary

Application
Understanding Jesus is the only one who can save you from sin

Response Activity
Trusting Jesus for salvation and thanking him for saving you from the punishment for sin

📖 BIBLE LESSON

■ Introduction

The importance of a name

Your name is important. It identifies who you are. We feel special when people remember our name. Sometimes we are named for a special person or because the name has a special meaning. ▲#5

Did you know that Jesus' name has a special meaning? It means *Savior*. ▲#6 God gave him that name because he came to be the Savior of the world. When we hear his name, it reminds us of what he did for us when he died on the cross and rose again. It reminds us of how powerful he is and that he can do what no one else can do. In our lesson we will see an example of his power.

■ Bible Content

1. A baby boy is born.
   (Acts 3:2; 4:22)

(Man 24, woman 25, baby 26)
Place all the figures on the board.
One day a baby boy was born in a little home in Jerusalem. The Bible doesn't tell us his name or about his childhood, but we can use our imagination to think about it.

He was probably welcomed and loved as all babies should be. But soon his mother and father noticed there was something wrong with his legs. He couldn't stand up and he never was able to walk. They must have felt sad and fearful,

▲ Option #5

Before class, have the children use markers or crayons to sign their names on a poster board or newsprint poster.
At this point, show the poster and have the children say their names aloud. As time permits, have them tell the meaning or background of their names or how they were chosen for them.

▲ Option #6

Definition word card:
JESUS / SAVIOR

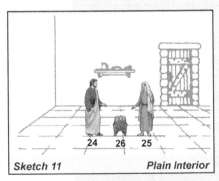

Sketch 11 — Plain Interior

for in those days there were no doctors who could help him, and life for a person who couldn't walk was very difficult. There was no wheel chair or special bus to take him where he wanted to go. He would have to be carried everywhere.

Sketch 12 — City Street

(Men 6D, man 27A, crowd 17)
When he became a man, the only way he could get money for food was to beg. So every morning friends carried him *(place 6D, 27A on the board)* to the temple and put him down beside one of the big gates. Every evening they carried him home again. Many people *(add 17)* passed through this gate all day long. Those who wanted to help him dropped a coin into his container. Everyone who came to the temple to worship knew him, for they saw him day after day, and year after year. At the time of our story he was a little more than 40 years old. *(Leave all the figures on the board.)*

2. Peter and John help the man who could not walk. (Acts 3:1-8)

Sketch 13 — City Street

(Peter 11, John 13, mat 27B, man 28A)
One day, when Peter and John *(add 11, 13)* were going to the temple to pray, they saw the man who couldn't walk sitting by the gate. The man saw them, too, and asked them for money.

Peter and John stopped and looked right at the man who was begging. Then Peter said, "Look at us!"

So the man looked up to them thinking, "Surely they are going to give me something."

But Peter surprised him. He said, "I don't have any money to give you, but I will give you what I have. In the name of Jesus Christ of Nazareth, walk."

Then Peter took the man by his right hand and helped him up. Instantly he *(remove 27A; add 27B, 28A)* jumped to his feet and began walking—for the first time in his life!

3. Peter witnesses to the crowd. (Acts 3:9-26)

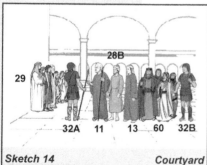

Sketch 14 — Courtyard

(Crowd 17, 29, man 28B, Peter 11, John 13, soldiers 32A. 32B)
Place 17, 29 on the board.
This happy, excited man *(add 28B)* went with Peter and John *(add 11, 13)* into the temple, walking and jumping and shouting, "Praise God, praise God, I can walk!"

Many people in the temple had seen him begging that very day. When they saw him walking and heard him praising

God, they were amazed and said to each other, "What has happened? How can this be?"

All the people came running to where the healed man was holding onto Peter and John. They wanted to know what had happened to make this man able to walk.

When Peter saw the great crowd of people, he said to them. "Why are you surprised? Why are you looking at us as though we healed this man by our own power? We didn't! God has glorified his Son Jesus by healing this man. You crucified Jesus, but God raised him from the dead. And this man was made strong and able to walk by faith in Jesus. That same power will save you if you turn to Jesus for the forgiveness of your sins."

4. The Jewish leaders put Peter and John in prison. (Acts 4:1-4)

The priests and some other leaders of the Jews heard that Peter and John were teaching the people about Jesus and the resurrection of the dead. They came right into the meeting bringing soldiers *(add 32A, 32B)* who arrested Peter and John and threw them into jail overnight *(remove 11, 13, 32A, 32B)*. Satan used the Jewish leaders to persecute the apostles.

But even though Peter and John were in jail, God's Word could not be stopped. Many other people believed in Jesus and were baptized. It had been only a few weeks since Jesus had gone back to heaven, but already there were at least 5,000 men who believed. Probably many women and children believed also.

5. The Jewish leaders threaten Peter and John. (Acts 4:5-21)

(High priest 33, Jewish leaders 31, 34, Peter 15, John 6E, soldier 32B, man 28A)

The next day the high priest *(place 33 on the board)* and the Jewish leaders *(add 31, 34)* who had condemned the Lord Jesus without a fair trial met together. They had Peter and John *(add 15, 6E, 32B)* brought from the jail. The man *(add 28A)* who had been healed was also there. The leaders began to question Peter and John: "By what power, or on whose authority, have you healed this man?"

Sketch 15   Council Room/Temple

Peter was filled with the Holy Spirit now and ready to suffer or die for the Lord Jesus. He stood before these wicked men and spoke boldly: "It is through the name of Jesus Christ of Nazareth, whom you crucified, but whom God raised from the dead, that this man standing before you is healed. There is no name under heaven by which we can be saved except Jesus' name."

These Jewish leaders knew that Peter and John had not gone to school for many years as many of them had. They could not understand how they could have such courage and speak so boldly, but they knew this change had come in them because of Jesus.

They sent Peter and John out of the room *(remove 15, 6E, 32B)*. Then they talked among themselves. "What can we do with these men? It is true that the healing of this man is a miracle. If we punish these men, the people will be very angry with us. But we must somehow stop them from talking about this Jesus, or more people will follow them."

Then they called Peter and John back into the room *(replace 15, 6E, 32B)* and said to them, "Do not speak or teach anymore in the name of Jesus."

Again Peter and John spoke boldly: "Do you think it is right in God's sight to obey you rather than God? We cannot help talking about the things we have seen and heard."

The leaders said, "We forbid you to teach in the name of Jesus. If you do it again, we will punish you severely." Then they let them go.

6. The disciples pray for boldness. (Acts 4:23-31)

Sketch 16   Plain Interior

(Peter 11, John 6E, disciples 6B, 6C, 6D)
Place 6B, 6C, 6D on the board.

When they were released, Peter and John *(add 11, 6E)* went at once to the other believers and told them all that had happened. Then they prayed together, "Oh, Lord, You know how these men have threatened us. Please help us to speak your word with great boldness." The most important thing to them was not to be kept safe, but to speak and teach boldly and so obey Jesus' last command. They were trusting in the Lord Jesus and in the power of his name.

■ Conclusion

Summary

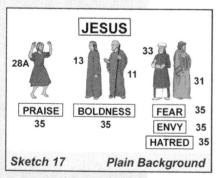

Sketch 17   Plain Background

(Man 28A, PRAISE, FEAR, ENVY, HATRED, BOLDNESS 35, Jewish leaders 31, 33, Peter 11, John 13)

Let's think about the people in our lesson and how they responded to the name of Jesus. What did the man who was healed *(place 28A on the board)* do after he was healed? *(Allow for response throughout.)* Yes, he praised God because he had been healed when he trusted in the name and power of Jesus *(add PRAISE 35)*.

How did the Jewish leaders *(add 31, 33)* react to the name of Jesus? That's right; they were filled with fear, envy and even hatred *(add FEAR, ENVY, HATRED 35[3])*. Why? Yes, because they refused to believe in who Jesus was or trust in his Name.

How did trusting in the name of Jesus help Peter and John? *(Add 11, 13.)* That's correct. God gave them power to heal the lame man and to speak boldly to the Jewish leaders who were so angry with them *(add BOLDNESS 35)*. They had courage in the face of danger.

What did Peter and John tell the people that Jesus' name had power to do besides heal? Yes, it has power to save those who trust in Jesus from the punishment for their sins. *(Have the children say Acts 4:12 together.)*

Application

(Word strip JESUS)

This message is for you and me today also. Which of these people are you like? Are you like the Jewish leaders *(point to 31, 33)* who up till then had refused to believe in the Lord Jesus *(add JESUS)*. Are you ready now to trust him to forgive your sin and save you? Just as the man *(point to 28A)* was healed through the name of Jesus, you may have salvation through his name.

Remember, to receive Jesus as your Savior, you must
- *Admit* you are a sinner, having done wrong things and displeased God.
- *Believe* that Jesus Christ is God, that he died on the cross for you, and that he rose again from the dead.
- *Choose* to receive Christ as your very own Savior and Lord.

If you have already believed in the Lord Jesus to save you from your sin, you are like Peter and John *(point to 11, 13)*. You are able to thank him for saving you. It is important for you to take the time each day to tell Jesus how glad you are for all he's done for you.

Response Activity

Distribute the **"Paper cross" handouts** and pencils. Have them print "JESUS" on the crossbar. Remind them that it is the only name that can save from sin's punishment. Show them your sample.

Have those who have already trusted Jesus as Savior print their name under Jesus' name and then pray sentence prayers thanking and praising Jesus for his wonderful name and for saving them.

Invite any who have not yet received Christ as their Savior to come and talk to you or a helper after class. Any who trust him then can print their names on their crosses at that time.

Encourage the children to use their crosses to remind them either to choose to trust in the name of Jesus for salvation or to thank him every day for saving them from the punishment for sin.

TAKE HOME ITEMS

Distribute **memory verse tokens for Acts 4:12** and **Bible Study Helps for Lesson 3**.

Ananias & Sapphira Lie to God
Theme: Holy Living

Lesson 4

❋ BEFORE YOU BEGIN...

"But it was only a little white lie. . . ." Living in a world that has become "open-minded" and "tolerant" of just about everything, we Christians have become desensitized to the awfulness of lying. We often fail to regard it as sin—even see it as a virtue if it seems to avoid an unpleasant consequence or help someone or protect another from being hurt. We seem to see lies on a scale of one to ten, with "small" ones being not as bad as "big" ones. Children are learning that if a lie doesn't hurt someone else or if they don't get caught, then it is not wrong.

In a very graphic manner the story of Ananias and Sapphira teaches us God's opinion of lying: it is sin and God hates sin! God is holy and he desires that his people live holy lives. He cannot and will not tolerate sin; he must punish it. Ask God to give you a new appreciation for his holiness and how our sin affects him. Then use this lesson to teach your children the seriousness of lying and the value of truth-telling. Teach them, as well, that God loves us so much that he made a wonderful way for us to be forgiven so we can escape the eternal punishment for sin. *"These six things the LORD hates, yes, seven are an abomination to him: a proud look, a lying tongue, hands that shed innocent blood, a heart that devises wicked plans, feet that are swift in running to evil, a false witness who speaks lies, and one who sows discord among brethren" (Proverbs 6:16-17, NKJV).*

☞ AIM:

That the children may

- Know that God is holy and wants his children to live a holy life.
- Respond by choosing to live a holy life by being truthful in all they say and do.

📖 SCRIPTURE: Acts 2:47; 4:32-37; 5:1-13.

♥ MEMORY VERSE: Proverbs 12:22

Lying lips are abomination to the Lord: but they that deal truly are his delight. (KJV)
The Lord detests lying lips, but he delights in men who are truthful. (NIV)

📁 MATERIALS TO GATHER

Memory verse visual for Proverbs 12:22
Backgrounds: Review Chart, Plain Background, General Interior, Plain Interior
Figures: 1R, R1-R4, 6C, 6D, 11, 13, 18, 23, 36(6), 37, 38, 39, 41, 43, 71
Token holders & memory verse tokens for Proverbs 12:22
Bible Study Helps for lesson 4
Special:
- **For Bible Content 1:** Picture of a church building; word strip CALLED OUT ONES
- **For Summary:** Word strips GOD, HOLY, HATES LYING; newsprint & marker or chalkboard & chalk
- **For Response Activity:** "To Tell the Truth" handouts, pencils
- **For Options:** Materials for any option you choose to use
- **Note:** Follow the instructions on page xii to prepare the word strips and the "To Tell the Truth" handouts (pattern P-4 on page 140).

REVIEW CHART

Display the Review Chart with 1R in place; have R1, R2, and R3 ready to use with the review questions. Add R4 when indicated. Use the following questions to review Lessons 1-3, repeating the memory verses as you add the building blocks.

1. Who is the foundation of our Life House? *(Christ; place R1 on chart.)*
2. Who gives us the power to live and witness for Jesus? *(The Holy Spirit; add R2.)*
3. What gift is given to us when we accept Jesus as our Savior from sin? *(Salvation; add R3.)*

When you look at a building, what parts of it do you see? *(Allow for response throughout.)* Which very important part do you usually not see? Yes, the foundation. What does the foundation do? Yes, it holds up the whole building. What would happen if the foundation were not strong? That's right; it would be leaning or falling down. How do we know that the building has a strong foundation? Yes, it is standing upright and its walls and roof are in the right places. ▲#1

It is the same with us and our Life House. The only way people will know we have Jesus Christ as our Foundation is by the life we live. The next block in our Life House describes the way God wants us to live when we have the Lord Jesus as our Foundation. *(Have a child read aloud the name on R4 and add it to the Chart.)* It is *Holy Living*.

The word *holy* means "clean and pure, without any sin." God is the only one who is truly holy. But his goal for you and me is that we

▲ **Option #1**

To show the importance of the foundation, mound some sand or soil on one side of a shallow box or tray and place a large rock on the other side. Set a small plastic or cardboard model of a house on the sand and pour water at its base to show how a weak foundation can cause a house to sink. Then place the house on the rock and repeat the process.

▲ **Option #2**

Have the children find the memory verse in their Bibles. If they have different translations, have it read aloud from each one.

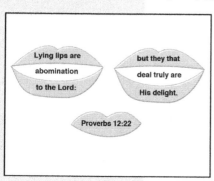

▲ **Option #3**

Memorizing the verse: Have the children read the verse aloud together. Then remove one piece of the verse visual. Allow a child who can say the verse with that piece missing to remove a second piece of the visual and hand it to you. Continue in this way until all the pieces of the visual have been removed.

Finally, have the whole class say the verse without visual help. Then distribute the visual pieces to any who did not participate in the first round and have them put the verse back on the board in correct order.

should live in such a way—a holy way—that others may see that the Lord Jesus is our Savior and is in control of all we say and do.

We can never be holy as God is holy while living here on earth. To live a holy life means for us to obey God's Word so that we will become more like the Lord Jesus in the way we live our lives. And because we have God the Holy Spirit in us, we have his power to help us do just that!

♥ **MEMORY VERSE**

Use the visual to teach Proverbs 12:22 when indicated.

Being truthful is one way we can show others that we are living in a holy way. Is it hard for you to tell the truth? *(Allow for response throughout.)* Did you ever tell something that wasn't true? Why did you lie? Was it to keep from being punished or was it to cover up someone else's actions? Did you get away with lying? Did telling the lie make things better? What happened when the truth was discovered? Perhaps you were never caught and think it's all right to lie. You might even think it is all right to lie if no one gets hurt or if other people are also saying things which are not true.

But what does God say about lying? Our memory verse gives us the answer to this question. *(Display the reference and the first part of the verse visual.)* ▲#2 As we read this part of our verse together, we will find a word which tells us what God thinks about lying. What is it? That's right; it is abomination (detests). Since God is holy, he hates lying and considers it disgusting.

Let's read the second part of our verse together *(display the last part of verse visual.)* How does God feel about those who are truthful? Yes, he is delighted—happy or very pleased—with us when we choose to obey his Word and tell the truth. *(Work on memorizing the verse.)* ▲#3

📖 **BIBLE LESSON OUTLINE**

Ananias & Sapphira Lie to God

■ **Introduction**

Jenny tells a lie

■ **Bible Content**

1. The Church is God's family on earth.
2. Ananias and Sapphira plan to lie to the apostles.
3. God punishes Ananias and Sapphira for lying.
4. The Church learns that God hates sin.

▪ Conclusion

Summary

Application
Learning how to deal with lying

Response Activity
Choosing to tell the truth

📖 BIBLE LESSON

▪ Introduction

Jenny tells a lie

Jenny was in trouble! She had borrowed her dad's new tennis racket without asking and now it was broken. She had thought she could practice with it and put it back without her dad finding out, but, of course, he had noticed that it was broken. And when he asked her if she knew anything about it, she lied! Finding out that the racket had been a special gift to her dad from a friend only made things worse.

Jenny thought she could avoid being caught and punished by lying. Instead, it only made more problems. Now she knew her dad would be very angry if he found out. She had to make up a good story. She hoped she could keep it all straight when Dad talked with her again.

To make matters worse, Jenny knew that lying is a sin. She had trusted Jesus as her Savior and wanted to please him. Still, she often found herself lying to keep out of trouble, thinking if no one found out or got hurt by her lie, it was all right. Was Jenny living in a holy way?

What should Jenny do? *(Allow for response throughout.)* ▲#4 What would God want her to do? *(Discuss how Jenny can live in a holy way now that she has lied and what she needs to do to make things right. Talk about why it would be difficult and what might happen as a result.)* Yes, Jenny needed to ask God to forgive her for lying, tell her dad the truth about what she had done and ask him to forgive her. That means she would have to be ready to take her punishment, not only for taking the racket without permission, but also for lying about what happened.

What might Jenny's parents think the next time they had to question her about something? Yes, it could be hard for them to trust her word until she continued to show them she was being truthful. What changes would Jenny have to make in order to live her life in a holy way in the future?

Today we will meet two people who thought they could get away with lying to God. Let's see what lesson they and the other believers learned from God about lying.

▲ **Option #4**

As time permits, have children dramatize various ways Jenny could respond to her problem.

Bible Content

1. The Church is God's family on earth. (Acts 2:47)

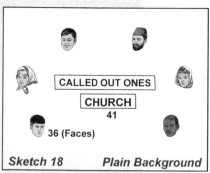

Sketch 18   Plain Background

(CHURCH 41, faces 36; picture of a church building, word strip CALLED OUT ONES)

When you see this word "CHURCH" *(place 41 on the board)* what picture comes to your mind? *(Encourage response.)* Most of us think of a building *(add the picture of a church)*. But the Bible meaning for this word is *called out ones (add CALLED OUT ONES)*. The Church is God's name for all those people who have put their trust in Jesus Christ as Savior. He has called them out of their old way of living to be part of his special family here on earth. ▲#5

The Lord Jesus is called the Head of the Church. His Church here on earth includes people of every color and race all across the world who are trusting in him for their salvation from sin. *(Add 36[6].)* They live in many different places and worship in many different kinds of church buildings, but they all belong to God's family and they all have Jesus as their Head or leader.

Pentecost, the day when the Holy Spirit came to live in believers, was the beginning of the Church on earth. The book of Acts tells us about the early Church and how it grew. As the apostles witnessed over and over about the death and resurrection of the Lord Jesus, many people believed in him and joined this big group of believers. Dr. Luke tells us that people were being saved and added to the Church every day (Acts 2:47). In a very short time after the Lord Jesus had gone back to heaven there were thousands who believed in him and belonged to his Church. ▲#6

Because God is holy, he wants his people to be holy, too. He wants to be proud of the people in his family. He wants unbelievers to see a "family likeness." Soon after the beginning of the Church God taught his people a lesson about his holiness and how he hates sin.

▲ **Option #5**

For younger children: Omit paragraph 3 from this section.

▲ **Option #6**

For older children, use Pattern P-17 on page 147 to draw a simple time line on newsprint or chalkboard to help them visualize the basic time periods.

2. Ananias and Sapphira plan to lie to the apostles. (Acts 4:32-5:2)

Sketch 19   General Interior

(Disciples 6D, 43, Peter 11, John 13, Ananias & Sapphira 37, Barnabas 6C)

Place 6D, 11, 13, 37, 43 on the board.

The people of the early Church were like one big family. They loved one another and shared what they had with each other. Some of them owned houses or lands. From time to time someone would sell a house or a piece of property and bring the money to the apostles to be used for any who were in need. One man who did this was named Barnabas *(add 6C)*.

(Ananias & Sapphira 37)
Apparently the other believers were impressed by the generosity of Barnabas, especially a couple named Ananias and Sapphira *(place 37 on the board).* ▲#7 One day they began talking together about selling a piece of their land and giving the money to the apostles. They must have been thinking more about what others would think when they saw them bring the money than of what God would think, because they planned to do something that displeased God very much.

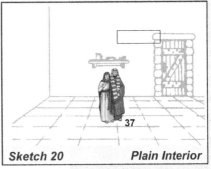

Sketch 20   Plain Interior

They sold the land and got the money. Then they agreed that they would keep part of the money for themselves and give only part of it to the Church. There was nothing wrong with that; they were not required to give any of it. The wrong thing was that they agreed to lie to the apostles, saying that they were giving all the money they had received for the land. The people watching them would think they were very generous and good.

3. God punishes Ananias and Sapphira for lying. (Acts 5:1-10)

(Apostles 6C, 6D, 43, Peter 11, John 13, Ananias 38, Sapphira 39)
Place 6C, 6D, 43, 11, 13 on the board.
So Ananias *(add 38)* brought the money to Peter and told him it was the full amount he and Sapphira had received for the land. He said that they wanted to give it to the Church.

But the Holy Spirit in Peter helped him to know that Ananias was not telling the truth. Peter said to him, "Ananias, why have you allowed Satan to fill your heart so that you have lied to the Holy Spirit? The land belonged to you. You did not have to sell it. And after you sold it, you could have kept all the money. Now you have done a terrible thing. You have not only lied to men, but you have lied to God."

Sketch 21   General Interior

When Ananias heard Peter say these words, he dropped dead instantly! Some of the younger men took his body *(remove 38)*, wrapped it in grave clothes and buried it immediately.

That was certainly a powerful display of God's holiness and shows how he punishes sin. The people who were watching were terrified. Perhaps they thought God was going to strike dead everyone who lied and they might be next! God doesn't usually choose to punish us immediately or as severely as he did Ananias. But he wanted the believers to know how serious sin really is, even for believers.

About three hours later Sapphira came in *(add figure 39)*. She did not know about the dreadful judgment that had fallen on her husband. Peter said to her, "Tell me how much you sold the land for. Was it for the amount that Ananias brought to me?"

"Yes," she replied, "that was the amount."

▲ Option #7

After telling the story of Ananias and Sapphira in abbreviated form, have the children dramatize it by:

1. acting the parts silently as verses 1-11 are read aloud; or

2. acting the parts, using their own dialog, as the text narrative is read aloud.

Note (1)

Why did God punish Ananias and Sapphira? Perhaps he wanted to teach the early Church an important lesson. Ananias and Sapphira thought they could put something over on God by masquerading as pious believers, but their hypocrisy and deception offended God's holiness. Also, he wanted to defeat Satan's plan to weaken the early Church through sin on the inside (Satan had filled Ananias' heart to lie, vs. 3), since he had failed to weaken it by persecution from the outside. But the Church emerged stronger as a result of the twin deaths (vss. 12-16).

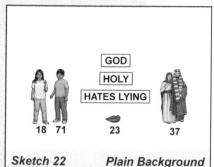

Note (2)

Be careful to differentiate between the lies and the liar. God loves his children "with an everlasting love," but he hates any lies they tell.

Then Peter said to her, "How could you agree to test the Spirit of the Lord by telling this terrible lie? Here come the men who buried your husband. They will carry you out too."

Immediately Sapphira fell down and died just as her husband had done. The young men came in, carried her body out *(remove 39)*, and buried it beside her husband. (1)

4. The Church learns that God hates sin. (Acts 5:11-13)

Word of what happened spread quickly through the Church, and even outsiders heard of it. Many became afraid when they knew that God saw and knew everything. They began to understand that God wanted his people to live holy lives.

Believers continued worshiping in the Temple court, but others were afraid to attend their meetings unless they were serious about receiving Christ as their Savior.

■ Conclusion

Summary

(Word strips GOD, HOLY, HATES LYING; newsprint & marker or chalkboard & chalk; lips 23, Ananias & Sapphira 37)

What two things have we learned about God *(Place GOD on the board)* in our lesson? *(Encourage response throughout.)* Yes, he is holy *(add HOLY)* and he wants his people to live holy lives. We have also learned that he hates lying *(add HATES LYING, 23)*. How did the believers in the early Church learn this? Yes, through what happened with Ananias and Sapphira *(add 37)*. What did they do? That's right; they lied to God by their words and actions. Were they living holy lives?

People lie in many ways. What are some of them? *(responses on newsprint or chalkboard. For example, not admitting they did wrong, telling a lie to keep from getting caught, pretending to be obedient when they're not or lying about someone else.)* ▲#8

What does God say about all of these lies? *(Say the memory verse together.)* He hates them! (2) When we lie we are not living holy lives or showing the holiness of God to others. What does God want us to do? Yes, he wants us to tell the truth.

Application

(Girl 18, boy 71; verse visual)

Does living a holy life mean that God expects us to be perfect? No, for we cannot be perfect on earth. He wants us to rely on his power to live a holy life. One way to do that is by asking God to help us tell the truth in everything we say and do.

What should a Christian do if he tells a lie? *(Response)* First, admit to God that he lied and ask for his forgiveness. God will forgive and make us clean from any sin that we confess to him (1 John 1:9).

Then we must admit to the person we lied to what we did and ask for forgiveness. Usually this is the hardest part, for we might have to be punished for lying or do something to make up for it. But if we don't admit we lied and tell the truth, they may not trust us or believe us when we *do* tell the truth. Then we may have to ask God for his help and power to stop telling lies. This is part of living a holy life.

How does God feel when we tell the truth? *(Display the verse visual and say the last part of the verse together.)* He is delighted! Even if it's difficult, we must learn to be truthful. God the Holy Spirit who lives in us will give us his power to tell the truth.

What about you? *(Add 18, 71.)* Do you need to tell God that you have told or lived a lie and that you are sorry? Will you ask God for his help and power to tell the truth in every situation?

Response Activity

Give the children an opportunity to confess in silent prayer any sin of lying and to thank God for his forgiveness. Talk with them about making things right with those to whom they have lied. Invite them to come after class to talk with you if they need to.

*Distribute the **"To Tell the Truth" handouts** and pencils. Have the children print on their card any time they have been tempted to lie but chose to delight God by telling the truth. If they cannot think of a time now, encourage them to record their response when they do face this temptation in the future.* ▲#9

Encourage any who have not trusted Christ as Savior to talk with you after class.

✍ TAKE HOME ITEMS

*Distribute **memory verse tokens for Proverbs 12:22** and **Bible Study Helps for Lesson 4**.*

▲ Option #8

Before class, write on cards some of the ways people lie, one to a card. Or write suggestions given by the class at this time on cards.

In class, divide the children into pairs or small groups. Give each of them one of the cards and have them prepare to act out what is written there. When each group has finished its scene, have the other groups tell how they lied and what the consequence might be.

▲ Option #9

Give each child a few smiley-face mini seals to take home with the card. Tell them to write on the card and/or attach a smiley-face sticker any time during the week when they are tempted to lie but instead choose to delight God by telling the truth.

The Apostles Are Put in Prison
Theme: Obedience

Lesson 5

 BEFORE YOU BEGIN...

Where is your priority? Obeying God or fitting in? Standing up for what you know is right or keeping peace with family and friends? Living by your convictions or keeping a low profile at work? Is it important to obey God's Word even when others oppose you? How can we stand up for what is right and true to God's Word when doing so may cause even our friends and family to become angry—or may cost our job?

This lesson provides important insights into God's plan for us when we are faced with these thorny questions at a time when absolutes seem to be vanishing. At stake for Peter and the other apostles was not only freedom, but also their very lives. But they stood firm and God helped them.

Help your children understand that God the Holy Spirit will give them the strength and power they need to obey God when it is very difficult. They may have families or teachers or friends who are actually hostile to God and his Word. They need to know that God is with them to help them stand for his truth, and that he will take care of them in it all. "Finally, my brethren, be strong in the Lord and in the power of His might" (Ephesians 6:10).

AIM:

That the children may

- Know that to please God they must obey him, even when it is hard.
- Respond by trusting God to help them obey in difficult situations.

SCRIPTURE: Acts 5:12-42

MEMORY VERSE: Acts 5:29

Then Peter and the other apostles answered and said, We ought to obey God rather than men. (KJV)
Peter and the other apostles replied: We must obey God rather than men. (NIV)

MATERIALS TO GATHER

Memory verse visual for Acts 5:29
Backgrounds: Review Chart, Plain Background, City Street, Prison, Council Room/Temple
Figures: 1R, R1-R5, 5, 6C, 6E, 6F, 7A, 11, 13, 15, 27A, 30, 31, 32A, 32B, 33, 34, 42, 44, 81
Token holders & memory verse tokens for Acts 5:29
Bible Study Helps for Lesson 5
Special:
- *For Introduction:* Small objects such as a pencil, small stone, feather, paper clip, straw
- *For Bible Content 4:* Newsprint & marker or chalkboard & chalk
- *For Summary:* Trinity circle(3 parts) from Lesson 2
- *For Application:* List from memory verse in Bible Content 4
- *For Options:* Materials for any options you choose to use

REVIEW CHART

Display the Review Chart with 1R in place. Place R1-R4 review pieces in random order on the table. As you review each memory verse, have a child choose the correct symbol to place on the Chart. Have R5 ready to use when indicated. Use the following questions to review Lesson 4.

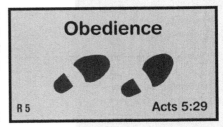

1. How does God feel about lying? *(It is an abomination; he hates it.)*
2. How did Ananias and Sapphira lie to God? *(By pretending they were giving the whole price of their land to God when they told Peter the property had been sold for the amount they brought in.)*
3. How did Peter know they were lying? *(God the Holy Spirit told him.)*
4. What happened to Ananias and Sapphira because they lied? *(They died.)*
5. What should we who believe in Jesus do when we sin by dying? *(Confess or admit it to God, ask him to forgive us, then make it right with the person we have hurt.)*
6. How can we show other people that we belong to the Lord Jesus? *(By obeying his Word and telling the truth.)*

The next building block for our Life House is called *Obedience* (place R5 on Review Chart). This word comes from another word you already know. It is the word *obey*. What does it mean to obey? *(Let children respond.)* It means to carry out instructions, to do what we are told. ▲#1

▲ **Option #1**

Definition word card:
Obedience = doing what we are told.

The Bible teaches us that when Jesus was here on earth he always obeyed God, his heavenly Father, as well as Mary and Joseph, his earthly parents. He is our example. It is important for us to obey God and our parents and those who are in authority over us. Our obedience pleases God. It also helps others see that we belong to God's family.

♥ MEMORY VERSE

Use the visual to teach Acts 5:29 in Bible Content 4.

📖 BIBLE LESSON OUTLINE

The Apostles Are Put in Prison

■ Introduction

An experiment with the law of gravity

■ Bible Content

1. The apostles heal many people.
2. Soldiers arrest the apostles.
3. An angel opens the prison doors.
4. Peter and the other apostles witness to the council.
    Memory verse presentation
5. Gamaliel gives good advice.
6. The apostles are beaten and released.

■ Conclusion

Summary

Application
Thinking about times when it is hard to obey

Response Activity
Asking God for help to obey

📖 BIBLE LESSON

■ Introduction

An experiment with the law of gravity

(Objects such as a small stone, pencil, paper clip, feather, straw)
Today we will conduct a small experiment to help us better understand what it means to obey. *(Ask different children to hold each of the objects in front of the class. At a given signal have them drop their objects to the floor as the other class members observe what happens.)*

▲ Option #2

1. Have the children, individually or in small groups, draw a picture illustrating *obedience*. Then give them time to show their illustration to the class and explain what it means.

2. Divide the class into pairs or small groups. Have them act out what it would mean to obey in one or more of the following situations—or in a situation they create.
   a. Being tempted to steal candy or toys from a store
   b. Being made fun of because they went to church on Sunday rather than to a soccer game
   c. Being tempted to cheat on a test
   d. Watching TV when mother is saying, "Do the dishes" or "Go to bed"

After each skit discuss with the class the choices the group had and which would show obedience to God. Also, discuss how the disobedience could be made right.

What happened to the objects? *(Encourage response throughout.)* Yes, they all landed on the floor, some more quickly than others. Why did all the objects do the same thing? Because they were obeying one of God's laws! Did you know that? Who knows which law it was? *(Children may have already given you this answer.)* Yes, the law of gravity. Why did they obey it? Because God made them to obey the law without question.

When it comes to obeying, how are these objects different from people? Yes, they have no choice; they have to "obey." People have no choice about obeying the law of gravity either. But God made us able to choose to obey or not to obey his laws in the Bible. God wants us to choose obedience to him and his Word, even when it is not easy and people make fun of us. The rules and commands he gives us are only for our good. He has also promised that God the Holy Spirit who lives in us will help us obey. ▲#2

In our lesson we will discover how God helped Peter and the other believers to choose to obey him in a very difficult situation.

■ Bible Content

1. The apostles heal many people.
(Acts 5:12-16)

(Disciples 6F, 13, 81, Peter 11, sick people 27A, 42)
Place 6F, 13, 81, 11 on the board.

After Ananias and Sapphira died because they had sinned by lying, the believers got serious about living for the Lord. They realized that being a believer in Jesus should not be taken lightly. Fear came upon all the Church as well as those who were not believers. Those who believed in the Lord Jesus understood that God is holy and that he wanted them to be holy, too.

Word spread all through the city of Jerusalem. God was doing some very special things to show his power and love. Relatives and friends carried sick people *(add 27A, 42)* into the narrow streets, which soon were filled with them lying on their mats waiting for Peter to pass by. The Bible says they were all healed! How they must have praised God and thanked him for his goodness! *(Leave all the figures on the board.)*

Sketch 23   City Street

2. Soldiers arrest the apostles.
(Acts 5:17, 18, 23)

(Jewish leader 30, soldier 32A)
When the Jewish religious leaders *(add 30)* heard about the wonderful things that were happening, they were filled with jealousy and anger. They had the apostles arrested *(add*

Sketch 24   City Street

🏠 **Note (1)**

If displaying the memory verse on the felt board, place the plain background between the Prison Background (Bible Content

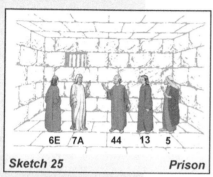

Sketch 25 — Prison

3) and the Council Room/Temple Background (Bible Content 4, 5, 6). When you complete Bible Content 3, flip both the Prison Background and

Sketch 26 — Council Room/Temple

the Plain Background to get to the Council Room/Temple Background for Bible Content 4. Then when you get to the memory verse, bring back the Plain Background, covering the Council Room/Temple with all the figures still there. When you remove the verse visual, flip the Plain Background to return to the Council Room/Temple

(continued on page 39)

32A) and thrown into the common prison, a dark and dirty place where criminals were kept.

3. An angel opens the prison doors. (Acts 5:19-21a)

(Peter 44, John 13, apostles 5, 6E, angel 7A)
Place 44, 13, 5, 6E on the board.
Perhaps Peter and the others remembered how the Lord Jesus had also been arrested and treated as a criminal. But during the night a wonderful thing happened. *(Have the children read Acts 5:15 to see what happened.)* An angel *(add 7A)* from the Lord opened the locked prison doors and led the apostles out. *(Remove all the figures.)* Then he said, "Go to the temple and tell the people all about this wonderful new life." So early in the morning, the apostles went to the temple and began to teach about Jesus.

4. Peter and the other apostles witness to the council. (Acts 5:21b-32)
Memory verse presentation

(Jewish leaders 33, 34, soldiers 32A, 32B, Peter 15, apostles 6C, 6E, Gamaliel 31)
Of course, the religious leaders *(place 33, 34 on the board)* knew nothing about the angel's visit. They thought the apostles were still in jail. The next morning they called the council together and sent officers to bring the apostles to stand trial before them. But the officers *(add 32A, 32B)* returned with a very strange story.

"We went to the prison," they said. "It was locked up tight and the guards were standing in their places. They unlocked the doors and we went in, but the men were all gone. No one knows how they got out. The guards were on duty all night long and saw no one."

The religious leaders were very puzzled and did not know what to do. While they were talking about it, someone rushed in, saying, "The men you put in prison yesterday are out in the temple court teaching the people again." Can you imagine how frustrated they must have felt?

So the leaders sent the officers again, this time with their captain, to bring the apostles before them. The soldiers did not want to use force because they were afraid the crowds of people would be angry and throw stones at them. They knew that many of the people loved the apostles and believed that what they were teaching about Jesus was true.

The apostles *(add 15, 6C, 6E)* went with the soldiers willingly. The leaders spoke roughly: "We gave you strict orders not to teach any more in the name of Jesus. Instead of obeying us, you are filling the whole city with your teaching and blaming us for the death of this Jesus."

Peter and the other apostles knew that these men were the ones who had put Jesus to death and could put them to death as well, but they answered boldly with the words of our memory verse *(leave all the figures on the board)*.

(Visual for Acts 5:29; newsprint & marker or chalkboard & chalk).

Display the verse visual. ◮**(1)**

As we read our verse together, think about what Peter and the others meant when they said these words to the Jewish leaders. *(Have the class read the verse together. Then have the boys read the first part and the girls, the second part.)* What does it mean to obey God rather than men or people? *(Allow for response throughout.)* Does it mean we should never obey anyone, even our parents or teachers, but only God? Not at all! The Bible teaches that we should be obedient to those who have authority over us.

But when should we refuse to obey someone? Yes, when they want us to do something that God's Word says is wrong. If we do that, we sin against God. Peter and the others knew they could not stop telling people about Jesus because he had told them to be witnesses for him.

Have friends ever wanted you to do something you knew God's Word said was wrong? What was it? *(Print their responses on newsprint or chalkboard. If necessary, prompt their thinking with an example such as a friend wanting them to give him answers to the homework assignment or to lie to their parents about why they were late or to do drugs or go shoplifting.)* ▲#**3**

Did you go along with them? What happened when you refused? Have others ever made fun of you so much that you finally gave in and disobeyed God just so they would stop? That's obeying people instead of God. *(Work on memorizing the verse.)* ▲#**4**

5. Gamaliel gives good advice. (Acts 5:33-40a)

Return to previous scene.

When Peter and the apostles said to the leaders, "We ought to obey God rather than men," they also witnessed about Jesus. "You killed Jesus by crucifying him," they said, "but God raised him from the dead. Now he's in heaven and can forgive your sins." When the leaders heard that, they became so angry that they wanted to kill all the apostles just as they had killed Jesus. "That's the only way we'll stop them!" they told each other.

But Gamaliel *(add 31)*, a wise man in the group, stood and said, "Send these men out of the room." *(Remove 15, 6C, 6E.)*

(continued from page 38)

for Bible Content 5 and 6. Then bring back the Plain Background the second time for the Summary.

▲ Option #3

As time permits, review the list you have made and discuss with children how they could obey God in each instance.

▲ Option #4

Memorizing the verse: Read the verse and reference aloud together. Have the children choose partners. Then give the pairs a few minutes to practice saying the verse to each other without looking at the visual.

Ask for a volunteer pair to stand and say the verse together from memory. Have that pair then choose another pair to do the same and so on until all have had an opportunity to say the verse.

You could also give each pair of children a piece of newsprint and markers to write the verse from memory.

Then he said to the rest of the council, "Leave these men alone. If God is with them you cannot stop them. If you try to do so, you will be fighting against God. If God is not with them, their teaching will die out all by itself."

The council had great respect for Gamaliel and knew that his advice was good. They agreed to do what he said, but they were determined to punish them. *(Leave all the figures on the board.)*

6. The apostles are beaten and released. (Acts 5:40b-42)

The apostles *(add 15, 6C, 6E)* were brought back to the council and beaten with heavy leather whips on their bare backs. The leaders commanded them again, "Do not speak any more in the name of Jesus." Then they let them go.

Even though their backs were bleeding from the terrible beating, the apostles rejoiced as they went on their way! They had obeyed God and God had allowed them to suffer for Jesus. Being beaten was a painful and shameful experience, but they did not complain. After all, hadn't Jesus been beaten for them only a few weeks before?

Do you think they obeyed the council and stopped teaching in Jesus' name? *(Response)* No! Every day they continued to teach and preach about Jesus in the temple and in homes. They were obeying God rather than men and they trusted God to take care of them.

■ Conclusion

Summary

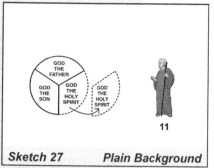

Sketch 27   Plain Background

(Peter 11; "Trinity" circle[3 parts])
What happened to Peter *(place 11 on the board)* and the apostles because they were teaching about Jesus and healing sick people in Jerusalem? *(Allow for response throughout.)* Yes, they were arrested. How did God help them in prison? That's right; he sent an angel to release them. What answer did Peter give to the Jewish leaders when they commanded them to stop preaching? Correct. Let's say our memory verse together. *(Do so.)* What did the leaders want to do to the apostles? Yes, they wanted to kill them. Did this stop the apostles from preaching about Jesus? No, it did not. How were they able to obey knowing they might be killed? That's right, God the Holy Spirit gave them the power to do it. *(Add Trinity circle; move Holy Spirit section toward Peter as indicated in the sketch.)*

Application

(List made from memory verse explanation)

Let's go back to the list we made of times when we should obey God rather than our friends. Would it be easy or difficult to obey God in each of these situations? *(As time permits, discuss each situation and why it would easy or hard to obey God in it.)* It isn't always easy to do what we know God wants us to do, for we may have to take punishment or teasing or even being ignored by our friends.

How can we be strong enough to stand up for what is right and obey God in really tough places? *(Response)* By depending on God the Holy Spirit to help us! If you are God's child, the Holy Spirit lives in you. Anytime you are faced with such a choice you can pray and ask him to give you strength and help.

Response Activity

Encourage those who have never trusted Jesus as Savior to receive him today so they can know that God the Holy Spirit lives in them to help them obey God. Invite them to come and talk with you about it after class.

Look at the list again. Ask the children to think of a situation on the list or in their own lives in which it is difficult for them to do what they know God wants them to do.

Have those who have trusted in Jesus pray, asking God to help them obey him in that situation during the coming week. Allow time for silent prayer.

Close the class by praying aloud, asking God to give each child his strength to obey in the situation they have chosen. Encourage the children to share next week how God helped them obey him.

✍ TAKE HOME ITEMS

Distribute **memory verse tokens for Acts 5:29** and **Bible Study Helps for Lesson 5.**

Stephen Dies for Jesus' Sake
Theme: Joy

Lesson 6

❋ BEFORE YOU BEGIN...

Every one of us is seeking for joy and peace. Where can we find them? And, if we find them, how can we keep them when life gets difficult? People attempt to meet this inner need through many avenues, such as relationships or career or wealth and possessions or fame and popularity—or by means of alcohol or drugs or sex or food or shopping. But none of these things can give real joy and peace.

Real joy and peace do exist! They are found in a personal relationship with God Himself. In Stephen we find a glowing example of one who experienced them in the midst of traumatic circumstances. Persecuted and martyred simply because he obeyed his Lord and bore a clear-cut witness for Jesus Christ, he died with forgiveness on his lips and joy on his face. Help your boys and girls understand that Stephen's joy came from God the Holy Spirit who lived within him. Teach them that they, too, can experience such joy in the midst of hard circumstances in their own lives if they have trusted Jesus as their Savior. *"These things I have spoken to you, that My joy may remain in you, and that your joy may be full"* (John 15:11, NKJV).

☞ AIM:

That the children may

- Know that God can give them joy when they are mistreated for obeying him.
- Respond by rejoicing when they are mistreated because of their witness for the Lord Jesus.

📖 SCRIPTURE: Acts 6:1–8:2

♥ MEMORY VERSE: Matthew 5:11

Blessed are ye, when men shall revile you and persecute you, and shall say all manner of evil against you falsely, for my sake. (KJV)

Blessed are you when people insult you, persecute you and false say all kinds of evil against you because of me. (NIV)

42

📁 MATERIALS TO GATHER

Memory verse visual for Matthew 5:11
Backgrounds: Review Chart, Plain Background, General Interior, City Wall, Council Room/Temple
Figures: 1R, R1-R6, 3, 6A, 6D, 6E, 6F, 6G, 6H, 7A, 7B, 11, 13, 14, 15, 16, 17, 24, 27A, 29, 30, 31, 33, 34, 37, 43, 44, 45, 46, 47, 48, 49, 50(2), 53, 60, 61, 81
Token holders & memory verse tokens for Matthew 5:11
Bible Study Helps for Lesson 6
Special:
- **For review Chart:** "Trinity" circle (Holy Spirit section) from Lesson 2; newsprint & marker or chalkboard & chalk
- **For Summary:** Word strips PEACE, JOY, FORGIVE
- **For Response Activity:** "Matthew 5:11" handouts, pencils
- **For Options:** Materials for any options you choose to use
- **Note:** Follow the instruction on page xii to prepare the word strips and the "Matthew 5:11" handouts (pattern P-5 found on page 141).

REVIEW CHART

Display the Review Chart with 1R in place. Distribute R1-R5 to individual children. Ask them to tell the meaning of their piece as they put it on the Review Chart. Review Lessons 1-5 by placing key figures from each lesson (suggested below) on the board. Then have the children take turns choosing a character(s) and giving a few facts about that figure.

Lesson 1 – Jesus 3, disciples 6D, 6E, angels 7A, 7B
Lesson 2 – Peter 15, crowd 17, Holy Spirit section from Trinity circle
Lesson 3 – Peter 11, John 13, man unable to walk 27A, Jewish leaders 34
Lesson 4 – Ananias & Sapphira 37, Peter 11
Lesson 5 – Angel 7A, disciples 13, 44, Jewish leaders 31, 33

Who would like to put our new building block on the Review Chart? *(Ask the volunteer to place R6 on the Chart and tell what block it is.)* What is joy? *(List the children's responses on newsprint or chalkboard.)*

Joy is a positive word and makes us think of happy times and happy feelings when things are going our way. Can you think of a time when you felt joy? *(Response)* But God's joy—the joy we are talking about today—is more than being happy. It is a special feeling deep inside that God gives to those who know Jesus as their Savior. It is a feeling of great gladness and deep happiness because we know that God loves us, will never leave us and will always be there to help us. We can have this joy even when we experience difficult or sad times in our lives. Our memory verse tells us why this is true.

▲ Option #1

Have the children find the verse in their own Bibles. If they have different translations, help them compare and understand the different wording.

▲ Option #2

Have the children give examples of some ways they might be mistreated for their belief in Jesus. (To trigger thinking, suggest something like being called names, left out of a group or teased.) Then have them describe how they should react or respond as believers.

♥ MEMORY VERSE

Display the visual for Matthew 5:11. Have the children read it aloud in unison. Then remove all pieces except the first one and the reference. ▲#1

Jesus spoke the words of our verse. In it he tells us some things that will happen. What is the first thing? *(Allow for response throughout.)* Yes, we will be blessed. *Blessed* means that God gives us good things and helps us through hard things, even bringing good out of them for us. Let's see *how* Jesus said we can be blessed by God.

Add the second visual piece and read it aloud in unison.

The word *revile (insult)* means *to deliberately say words that hurt someone.* Does Jesus mean that being hurt by another because we obey him is a blessing from God? Let's read on.

This also sounds like a strange way to be blessed *(add the third visual piece and have someone read it aloud).* The word *persecute* means *to treat people badly,* by beating or hurting them, by saying bad things to or about them or by ignoring them. What do you think Jesus meant?

What do you think this part means? *(Add the fourth visual piece and read it aloud together.)* Jesus was saying that people will lie and tell wrong things about us when we choose to live for him and obey God's Word. That doesn't sound very much like a blessing either.

But we have one last piece and it tells us why people will say and do these things to us *(add the fifth visual piece and read it aloud together).* Is Jesus saying that these things will happen to us because we have hurt others or said wrong things about them? No, Jesus is saying it may happen because we stand up for what we believe about Jesus and obey him. ▲#2

Now go back to the first part of the verse. What did Jesus say will happen? We will be *blessed* in all of this. How does God bless us when we are going through persecution for him? *(Allow for response and discussion.)* God *blesses* us by helping us and by giving us his power to do what is right even when it is very difficult. He also *blesses* us by giving us his joy and peace in the middle of being hurt or lied about by others.

Who remembers how God blessed the apostles in last week's lesson? Yes, he gave them power to act bravely and speak boldly for him. God can give us exactly the same courage and boldness to face those who would mistreat us for standing true to God and his Word. *(Work on memorizing the verse.)* ▲#3

📖 BIBLE LESSON OUTLINE

Stephen Dies for Jesus' Sake

■ Introduction

Ben makes a choice

▪ Bible Content

1. The Church continues to grow.
2. Stephen witnesses for Jesus.
3. Lying witnesses speak against Stephen.
4. Stephen dies for Jesus.

▪ Conclusion

Summary

Application
Being mistreated for our faith

Response Activity
Rejoicing when being mistreated

📖 BIBLE LESSON

▪ Introduction

Ben makes a choice ▲#4

Ben was really afraid! He had said no when his friends wanted him to help them steal. Now they were very angry with him. They even had some tough kids threaten him.

It all began when Ben's friends decided to steal some sports equipment from the neighbor's garage. After all, their neighbor never used it and they really needed it for their games. They figured out how to do it and even planned the lie they would tell to hide what they had done. Then they asked Ben to help them.

But a year earlier Ben had trusted Jesus as his Savior and he knew that God's Word says, "You shall not steal." He really wanted to obey God, but he didn't want to lose his friends and have no one to play sports with. It was a tough choice, but he had to say no.

When he refused to go along with them, they threatened to hurt him—especially if he told on them. They said he couldn't play with them ever again. They called him names and turned the kids in school against him. Now he was not only sad, but scared! What would happen next? *(You will return to this question for discussion in the Application.)*

It's hard to suffer for doing the right thing—for obeying God when everyone else seems to be against you. Do you know there are people in many countries today who are in jail or being tortured or even put to death because they believe in God and choose to obey him? Even in our own country children and adults sometimes suffer because they believe in Jesus and stand up for what is right.

In our lesson today we will learn about a man who was put to death for believing in Jesus. Listen to discover how he reacted to those people who hurt him.

▲ Option #3

Memorizing the verse: Choose six children to hold the verse visual in front of the class as everyone reads the verse aloud. Then have one of those children sit down. Ask for a volunteer to say the verse without that piece. Continue until all the children are seated.

Then have them put their pieces on the table in random order. Allow other class members to put pieces back on the board in correct order, with the class saying the complete verse in unison each time a piece is added.

Finally, remove all visual pieces and say the verse again.

▲ Option #4

Before class, prepare several children to act out Ben's story, using their own dialogue or as you read it aloud. After their presentation, have the group discuss and/or demonstrate some possible endings to the situation; for example, Ben giving in to friends or obeying God.

■ Bible Content

1. The Church continues to grow. (Acts 6:1-7)

Sketch 28 — General Interior

(Disciples 6A, 14, 43, 81, Peter 11, Philip 6E, Stephen 24) Place all the figures on the board.

The Church kept growing in Jerusalem because more and more people came to believe in Jesus as Savior. You will remember that they all shared what they had so that no one was in need. In the Church there were many women whose husbands had died. Some of them were not able to work and earn money for themselves. Every day Peter and the other apostles would see that food was given to them and to any others who needed it.

Then one day Peter and the other apostles called all the believers together and said, "It is important to care for the widows, but we apostles don't have time to do it. It's not right for us to neglect preaching the Word of God in order to give out the food. Let's choose seven men who are filled with the Holy Spirit (which means the Holy Spirit was able to work through them because they were willing to obey him) and very wise. They can give out the food and help these people. We will do our work of praying and preaching the Word of God."

The whole group thought this was a good idea, so they chose Stephen and six other men who were strong in their faith and obedient to the Holy Spirit. The apostles then placed their hands on the heads of these seven men and prayed that they would do their work faithfully.

So the Word of God continued to spread. And the number of believers in Jerusalem increased rapidly. Even many of the Jewish priests believed in Jesus!

2. Stephen witnesses for Jesus. (Acts 6:8-12)

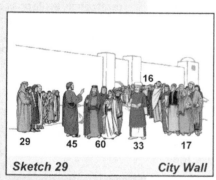

Sketch 29 — City Wall

(Stephen 45, crowds 16, 17, 29, Jewish leader 33, people 60)

Stephen *(place 45 on the board)* was known and loved by everyone in the Church. Find Acts 6:8 in your Bible and read it silently. What does verse 8 tell us about Stephen? *(Response)* Yes, he was full of God's grace and power. And he did wonderful things. Stephen loved to tell people *(add 16, 17, 29, 33)* about Jesus' death and resurrection. God helped him do some amazing miracles in Jesus' name among the people, so they would believe in Jesus as God's Son and their Savior.

But not everyone liked this. God was working in the hearts of many people to turn them to Jesus, but Satan was working too. He did not want the people to hear about Jesus or believe in him, so he caused some of the Jewish people *(add 60)* to argue and debate with Stephen.

God the Holy Spirit helped Stephen answer them with such wise words that they could not find anything wrong in what he said. This made them very angry. They were determined to stop him, so they persuaded some men to tell lies about him. Then they stirred up a great crowd of people, who grabbed Stephen and brought him before the council of Jewish leaders. This was the same group of men who condemned Jesus to death and later commanded Peter and the other apostles not to teach or preach anymore in the name of Jesus.

3. Lying witnesses speak against Stephen. (Acts 6:13—7:56)

(Council 30, 31, 34, men 61, Stephen 45)
Place all the figures on the board.

The lying witnesses said to the council, "This man is always teaching wicked things against the law and trying to change our customs. We have heard him say that Jesus of Nazareth will destroy this holy place. He is contradicting what Moses taught our people many years ago. This dishonors God."

How did Stephen react when these men lied about him? Let's look at verse 15. The men on the council were watching him closely. What did they see? They saw that his face looked like the face of an angel. ▲#5

Sketch 30 Council Room/Temple

Perhaps it was very peaceful and glowing. God gave him special joy and peace deep inside even though he was being treated badly.

The high priest said to Stephen, "Are these things true?"

Stephen answered by talking about some of the great men that God had sent to their nation years before. These men on the council were familiar with all of them. He spoke of Abraham whom God had chosen to be the father of the Jewish people to which they all belonged. He reminded them of Joseph and how God watched over him in the land of Egypt after his brothers had sold him into slavery.

He then talked about Moses, the great leader God used to deliver the Israelites from slavery in Egypt. Yet those very same people would not listen to Moses and made things difficult for him. They even made a golden calf to worship instead of the true and living God.

Then Stephen reminded them of how God had sent many messages to the Jewish people through the prophets, and how the Jews had persecuted many of the prophets and killed others.

Stephen ended his talk by saying, "Our fathers did all these wicked things and would not listen to God or obey him. You are just like them. You betrayed the special person God sent to you and killed him." Of course, he was talking about Jesus.

When the men on the council heard Stephen say these things they became so angry that they ground their teeth together, shook their fists and shouted at him. ▲#6 They hated what he said about Jesus and

▲ **Option #5**

For younger children, say to the class, "Show me what you think his face looked like."

▲ **Option #6**

For younger children, say to the class, "What do you think their faces looked like? Show me. Do you think they had the peace and joy Stephen had?"

▲ Option #7

If your children need teaching about what death means for the believer, prepare the body/soul/spirit circles as explained below. Place them above Stephen on the board as you teach the following information.

God has made each of us a complete person (place

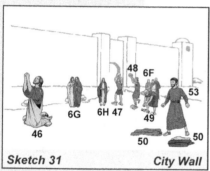

Sketch 31   City Wall

PERSON circle on the board) with three parts —a body, a soul and a spirit (place body, soul and spirit sections on PERSON circle). Your body is the part that other people see, the part you can feel, see, move and taste with. The soul is the real you inside that no one else sees, the part of you that thinks and feels and makes choices. The spirit is the part of you that can know and love God. It is also where God can live within you.

If you have accepted Jesus as your Savior, when your body dies your soul and spirit go immediately to be with God in heaven (move soul and spirit sections upward). What a wonderful hope that is for us who know and believe

(continued on page 49)

themselves. But Stephen did not even seem to see them. He was looking upward toward heaven.

"Look," he cried, "I see heaven open and the Son of Man standing at God's right side." When the Lord Jesus went back to heaven, he sat down at God the Father's right side. But now he was standing to encourage Stephen as he was being persecuted and to welcome him home to heaven. ▲#7

4. Stephen dies for Jesus.
(Acts 7:54-60; 8:2)

(Crowd 6F, 6G, 6H, Stephen 46, men with stones 47, 48, 49, garments 50[2], Saul 53)

The men didn't want to hear this. Covering their ears, they shouted at the top of their voices and dragged him out of the room and through the city streets. When they got outside the city walls *(place 6F, 6G, 6H, 46, 47, 48, 49 on the board)*, they pulled off their coats and gave them to a young man named Saul to hold *(add 50[2], 53)*. Then they began throwing stones at Stephen.

Look in verses 59 and 60 to see what Stephen did. What do you find? *(Response)* Yes, he looked up to heaven and prayed, "Lord Jesus, receive my spirit." He knew he was going to die and he knew where he was going.

What else did Stephen pray? Look in verse 60. *(Response)* That's right, he prayed in a loud voice, "Lord, do not hold this sin against them." Even when the men were murdering him Stephen did not think of himself. Like Jesus, who on the cross prayed for those who crucified him, Stephen prayed for those who were stoning him and asked God to forgive them.

After that, Stephen died! His soul and spirit left his body and went to heaven to be with the Savior he loved.

The Jewish leaders were glad when Stephen was dead. Now they would not have to listen to his words about Jesus. But his friends were very sad. They buried his body and they cried when they thought of how he had been killed. But the Lord gave them hope and joy deep in their hearts when they remembered that Stephen's soul and spirit had gone to heaven to be with Jesus.

Stephen was the first one to die because he believed in Jesus and obeyed him. He is called a martyr. A martyr is one who dies for what he believes. Since that time many people who believe in Jesus have been martyred because they had faith in him, obeyed his Word and were not afraid to tell others about him.

■ Conclusion

Summary

(Stephen 45; word strips PEACE, JOY, FORGIVE)
Why was Stephen *(place 45 on the board)* persecuted and then killed by the Jewish leaders? *(Allow for response throughout.)* Yes, he was telling them God's truth about Jesus and about themselves and they didn't want to hear it.

Who remembers how Stephen acted when he was treated wrongly? What did the men think his face looked like? Yes, like an angel's. He had peace and did not fight back or get angry *(add PEACE)*. Instead, he kept on telling them about Jesus. When he had finished speaking and the men became so angry, what did Stephen see? Yes, he saw heaven open and Jesus standing at God's right side. This filled him with joy *(add JOY)* because he knew he was obeying God.

When Stephen was being stoned to death, what incredible thing did he do? Yes, he asked God to forgive *(add FORGIVE)* the men who were killing him! How could he do that? He could do it because he was trusting in the Lord Jesus and God the Holy Spirit was making him strong. Stephen knew that if he died, he would immediately go to live with Jesus forever.

Sketch 32   Plain Background

Application

(Matthew 5:11 visual)
Today there are some places in the world where people are not permitted to become believers in Jesus *(display verse visual)*. In fact, if their government authorities find out that they have trusted in Jesus, they may punish them severely, put them in jail or even put them to death.

You and I may never be beaten or killed for believing in Jesus, but there are other ways people can mistreat us because of our faith. Remember what happened to Ben at the beginning of our lesson? *(Review how Ben's friends treated him; discuss how the situation might have ended, whether good or bad.)* Has anything like that ever happened to you?

How did Ben feel when his friends treated him like that? How would you feel? *(Response)* Sometimes we feel angry or hurt and we want to get even or fight back, but God says we are not to do these things. Instead, he can give us power to walk away and not get angry. He can give us joy and peace just like He gave Stephen. He can even help us pray for those who hurt us. Then those who mistreat us will see that it is Jesus Christ in our lives who gives us that joy and strength.

Let's say our verse together to remind us of what Jesus said would happen if we follow him and live for him.   ▲#8

(continued from page 48)

in Jesus, even when we are mistreated for loving him.

To make body/soul/spirit circles, cut two circles from flannel or felt. Print PERSON on one. Divide the other into three equal parts like a pie. Print BODY on one section, SOUL on the second section, and SPIRIT on the third. Cut the sections apart.

▲ Option #8

Act out some of the situations where children might be mistreated for their faith. (See Option #2.)

Put the children in pairs or small groups. Have each group prepare and act out a skit depicting one of the situations you have discussed or one they make up themselves. Then discuss how we should respond in each one.

Response Activity

Explain to the children that they cannot experience God's joy until they have received the Lord Jesus Christ as Savior. Invite any who have never trusted Jesus as Savior to do so now.

Distribute the **"Matthew 5:11" handouts** and pencils. Give them time to print their names on the line after the word "you." Then ask them to think of a time when they were mistreated because they did what Jesus wanted them to do and print that on the next line. Encourage them to rejoice by reading aloud what they have printed and telling about their experiences and how they reacted.

If children have never had such an experience, let them take their papers home and print on them when they are mistreated for obeying Jesus.

Remind everyone of two things: 1) That we are to rejoice and feel privileged to go through hard times when we do it for Jesus, and 2) that we should pray for those who mistreat us, asking God to help us forgive as Stephen did.

Close in prayer, asking God to help each one to be faithful to him even when it is hard.

TAKE HOME ITEMS

Distribute **memory verse tokens for Matthew 5:11** and **Bible Study Helps for Lesson 6**.

Philip Obeys the Word of God
Theme: God's Word

Lesson 7

✻ BEFORE YOU BEGIN...

Today's children are being bombarded with options and choices—from cereals to clothing to computer games; from lifestyle standards to future careers. They need to know that God's Word contains guidelines and insights that will give them direction and steady them as they grow and develop into the people God intends for them to be. They need to be aware that everything God has to say is up-to-date and relevant for life in our "modern" world. And they need to understand that every choice they make affects someone else, as did Philip's choice to obey God when it didn't make sense to go down to the desert. His meeting with the Ethiopian would have far-reaching effects on the continent of Africa.

Impress upon your children the importance of looking to God's Word for guidance in their daily life. Use this lesson to help them make a commitment to read God's Word and obey it. Such a commitment will pay rich dividends. *"How can a young man cleanse his way? By taking heed according to Your word. With my whole heart I have sought You; oh, let me not wander from Your commandments!" (Psalm 119:9-10, NKJV).*

👉 AIM:

That the children may

- Know that God is speaking to them whenever they read the Bible or hear it taught.
- Respond by discovering what God says to them in his Word and then obeying it.

📖 SCRIPTURE: Acts 8:1-8, 26-39

♥ MEMORY VERSE: Luke 11:28

Blessed are they that hear the word of God and keep it. (KJV)
Blessed rather are those who hear the word of God and obey it. (NIV)

▲ Option #1

Show a children's video with God's Word being read or dramatized or sung. Display several Bible story books; allow time for children to look at them.

📁 MATERIALS TO GATHER

Memory verse visual for Luke 11:28
Backgrounds: Review Chart, Plain Background, General Interior, City Street, General Outdoor
Figures: 1R, R1-R7, 3, 5, 8(2), 17, 25, 27A, 29, 32A, 42, 53, 54A, 54B, 55(2), 56, 57, 81
Token holders & memory verse tokens for Luke 11:28
Bible Study Helps for Lesson 7
Special:
- *For Introduction & Application:* "God's Word" chart, marker
- *For Bible Content 2:* MAP OF ISRAEL
- *For Response Activity:* "God's Word" handouts, pencils
- *For Options:* Materials for any options you choose to use
- *Note:* To prepare the "God's Word" chart, duplicate the chart found on page 54 onto newsprint or chalkboard. Fill in the verse references, but only the first line under "God Says" as an example of what you expect. Leave the "I need to obey" lines blank to fill in with the children. Follow the instructions on page xii to prepare the Map of Israel, (pattern P-1 on page 138) and the "God's Word" handouts (pattern P-6 on page 141).

🏠 REVIEW CHART

Display the Review Chart with R1 in place. Have R1-R6 ready to use with the review questions. Review Lessons 1-6 by having the children answer the questions with the appropriate memory verse. Allow the child who gives the verse to place its symbol on the Chart and then say the verse again with the rest of the class. Have R7 ready to use when indicated.

1. What promise was given to the disciples after Jesus went back to heaven? *(Acts 1:11)*
2. How do we get power to obey God's Word? *(Acts 1:8)*
3. Through whose name can we be saved? *(Acts 4:12)*
4. What does God say about lying lips? *(Proverbs 12:22)*
5. Whom does God say we should obey? *(Acts 5:29)*
6. What does God give to those who suffer for Jesus sake? *(Matthew 5:11)*

♥ MEMORY VERSE

Display the visual to teach Luke 11:28.
The new building block for our Life House is found in our memory verse. Read carefully to see if you can discover

what it is. Yes, it is the Word of God or *God's Word*. *(Have the children read the verse aloud together; place R7 on the Chart.)* Where do we find God's Word? *(Allow for response throughout.)* That's right; it's in the Bible. The Bible is God's written Word to us.

Our verse tells us two things we are to do with the Word of God. What are they? Yes, to *hear* it and *keep (obey)* it.

How can we *hear* God's Word? *(If necessary, prompt thinking with examples such as hearing someone read it on TV or radio, in Sunday school or Bible Club, or watching a video, or by reading the Bible ourselves.)* ▲#1

Can we *hear* the Word of God by reading or studying it ourselves? Yes, for we can hear it in our minds as we read even though there is no audible sound. ◨(1)

We should first *hear* what God is saying and then *obey* it. We must listen carefully to God's Word—even memorize it as we do in class. Then we must obey it or do what it tells us to do.

What does our verse say will happen if we hear and obey God's Word? Yes, we will be *blessed*. Who remembers what the word *blessed* means? Yes, God blesses us by helping us and giving us his power to do what is right even if it is difficult or we may not feel like it. He also blesses us by giving us joy when we do what is right. God the Holy Spirit living in us will help us do what God's Word tells us to do and we will grow stronger spiritually. And then he will give us joy because we have obeyed. We really need God to bless us because some of the things he tells us to do are not easy to do. *(Work on memorizing the verse.)* ▲#2

📖 BIBLE LESSON OUTLINE

Philip Obeys the Word of God

■ Introduction

What is God saying?

■ Bible Content

1. The believers in Jerusalem obey God's Word.
2. The Samaritans obey God's Word.
3. Philip obeys God's Word.
4. The Ethiopian obeys God's Word.

■ Conclusion

Summary

Application
Understanding God wants you to read and obey his Word

Response Activity
Reading the Bible and obeying what it says

◨ Note (1)

When we use the expression "hearing God's Word" or "God speaking through his Word," we do not just mean listening with our ears when the Bible is read or taught to us. Rather, we are referring to God's communication to us in a way that is as real as if he were talking with an audible voice. God reaches us in our minds so that we can respond as if he were talking to us. Our ears are bypassed, but the impression on our minds is the same.

Developing the skill of "hearing God's voice" in this way is a dire necessity if we are to respond obediently to God's will. And it is equally as important that we help our students to develop this skill so they can discern between God's voice and devilish thoughts or self-made ideas. Every idea needs to be tested by what God's Word says.

▲ Option #2

Memorizing the verse: Read the verse aloud several times: the whole class, the boys, the girls. Then have the teacher(s) and children take turns personalizing the verse and saying it for the class: "Blessed [is Tommy who] hears the Word of God and keeps it." Finally, have the class close their eyes and say the verse together.

▲ **Option #3**

1. Use the verses on the "God's Word" chart as a Bible drill.

To conduct a Bible drill:
Have the children hold their Bibles in both hands in front of them.
Give the reference to find: e.g., John 1:12.

Have the children repeat the reference together. Give the command, Go! Have the first one to find the verse, stand and read it. To make it a contest, have those who find the first six verses come to the front. Give the final verse to them to determine the winner.

2. *For younger children,* choose two or three of the verses and print them on newsprint or chalkboard for all to read.

📖 **BIBLE LESSON**

■ **Introduction**

What is God saying?

We learned in our memory verse that we will be blessed if we hear God's Word and then obey it. Perhaps you really want to obey God but wonder just what he wants you to do. We're going to use this chart today to help us find the answer to that question. *(Display the "God's Word" chart you have prepared.)*

First we'll find and read the Bible verses listed under "God's Word." Then we'll talk about what God is saying we should do and print that under "God says." *(Have the class as a whole look up the verses, or assign them to individual children. As each verse is read aloud, have the children decide what God is saying and how to fill in the "God Says" column. If you need to save time in class, fill in the "God Says" column ahead of time and cover each answer with a strip of paper secured by small rolls of transparent or masking tape. Remove each strip when the answer is needed. Leave the "I Need to Obey" column to be completed during the Application.)*

God's Word	God Says	I need to obey:
John 1:12	Receive Jesus as Savior	_____
Ephesians 6:1	Obey parents	_____
Ephesians 4:32	Be kind, forgive others	_____

Note: Use these verses or choose others that fit the needs of your class. ▲#3

Now that you know what God is saying in these verses, what do you think he wants you to do? *(Response)* Yes, God wants you to obey him. We will talk about how we can do that later in our lesson. Listen carefully to today's Bible story to learn who obeyed God's Word.

■ **Bible Content**

1. **The believers in Jerusalem obey God's Word. (Acts 8:1-4)**

(Jesus 3, words 8[2], Saul 84)
Just before Jesus *(place 3 on the board)* went back to heaven he gave his disciples two commands. What were they? *(Response)* Yes, they were to WAIT *(add WAIT 8)* in Jerusalem for the Holy Spirit to come. And they were to GO *(add GO 8)* to all the world to preach the gospel.

We've been learning how the apostles and the other believers boldly witnessed about Jesus' death and resurrection in Jerusalem even when they were put in prison for it. God

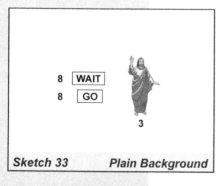

Sketch 33   Plain Background

was honored, many people believed and the Church grew rapidly. That was the first command.

But the Lord Jesus' second command still needed to be obeyed. God allowed the believers to be persecuted so they would leave their homes and take the message of Jesus' death and resurrection to other parts of the world. You remember that Stephen was stoned to death because he believed in Jesus and dared to preach about him. *(Remove 8, 8[2].)*

A young Jewish man named Saul *(add 84)* was there the day that Stephen was stoned. He believed in God and was trained to be a leader. He didn't throw any stones at Stephen, but he showed whose side he was on by watching over the coats of those who did throw stones. Like the other Jewish leaders, he believed that Jesus was not God's Son or the Savior. In fact, he was determined to keep other people from believing in Jesus, and so he became a strong persecutor of believers. *(Remove 3, 8[2].)*

▲ **Option #4**

Have several children read Acts 8:8 from different translations, or print the verse on newsprint or chalkboard for all to read together.

(Man 5, woman 25, soldier 32A, Saul 84; MAP OF ISRAEL) Place 5, 25 on the board.

With his helpers Saul *(add 32A, 84)* went from house to house in Jerusalem arresting men and women who believed in the Lord Jesus and putting them into prison. The believers soon heard about this and, except the apostles, packed up their and moved away. As they went to new places, they obeyed Jesus' command to teach and witness for him. So the good news was carried from Jerusalem to Judea and Samaria and into other parts of the world as the Lord had commanded them. *(Indicate on the map.)*

Sketch 34   General Interior

2. The Samaritans obey God's Word. (Acts 8:5-8)

(Philip 81, crowds 17, 29, men 27A, 42; MAP OF ISRAEL)

Philip was one of the believers who left Jerusalem during the persecution. He had been Stephen's friend and was chosen along with Stephen to be one of the seven men who would take care of the poor people. He too was filled with the Holy Spirit—wise and strong in his faith in Jesus.

Philip *(place 81 on the board)* went to Samaria *(indicate on the map)* and preached about the Lord Jesus. Some of those people may have seen Jesus and heard him preach when he was there a few years before.

Sketch 35   City Street

Great crowds *(add 17, 29)* listened carefully as Philip preached God's Word. They saw God's power working through Philip as he performed many miracles, healing sick people *(add 26A, 42)* and casting out evil spirits. What was the result? Let's read Acts chapter 8, verse 8 to find out. *(Have the children find this verse in their Bibles and respond.)* Yes, there was great joy in that city.   ▲#4

◪ **Note (2)**

Angels are spirit beings created by God to serve him in heaven and throughout the universe. They are invisible so can only be seen when they take a visible form. Most often in the Bible angels act as God's messengers, as in today's Bible story. Colossians 1:16; Hebrews 1:14; Psalm 103:20.

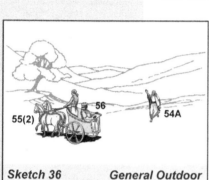

Sketch 36   General Outdoor

▲ **Option #5**

Use a world map to show the location of Ethiopia in Africa and how far it is from Israel.

Sketch 37   General Outdoors

3. **Philip obeys God's Word.**
   (Acts 8:26-28)

(MAP OF ISRAEL)
One day an angel ◪(2) spoke to Philip. Look in verse 26 to see what the angel said. *(Have one child read the verse aloud.)* Yes, he was to leave Samaria and go down to a desert road that went from Jerusalem to Gaza *(locate on the map).*
Gaza was about 60 miles from Samaria—a long way to walk or even ride a donkey. Perhaps Philip wondered why God was sending him to the desert. Would there be any people there? Do you think Philip obeyed God? Look in verse 27 to find out. *(Let children respond.)* Yes, he did. He did not question God or argue with him. He got up and went south into the desert as he had been told.

(Philip 54A, chariot & driver 55[2], Ethiopian 56)
As Philip walked along the hot, desert road *(place 54A on the board)*, he saw a man from Ethiopia—a country in Africa—riding along in a chariot *(add 55[2], 56).* This man was an important official in that country, in charge of all the queen's treasures—her silver, her gold and her jewels. Probably many servants were traveling with him.   ▲#5
The people of Ethiopia worshiped many idols, but this man had heard of the one true God. He had made the long journey to Jerusalem to worship God. Now he was going back home. As they traveled along, he was reading aloud from the book of Isaiah, one of the Old Testament books in the Bible. *(Leave all the figures on the board.)*

4. **The Ethiopian obeys God's Word.**
   (Acts 8:29-39) ◪(3)

(Philip 54B)
The Holy Spirit spoke to Philip: "Go over to that chariot."
So Philip ran up to the chariot. *(Move 54A near to the chariot.)* As he came near, he heard the man reading aloud, *(have a child read the words from verse 32)* "He was led as a lamb to the slaughter and as a sheep before her shearers is dumb, so he opened not his mouth" (Isaiah 53:7, 8).
Philip called out, "Do you understand what you are reading?"
"How can I," the Ethiopian replied, "unless someone explains it to me?" Then he invited Philip to sit with him in the chariot *(remove 54A; add 54B).*
"I don't understand this," he said. "Is the prophet talking about himself, or about someone else?" ◪(4)
As they rode along, Philip used the verses in Isaiah to explain the good news about Jesus' death and resurrection. The Bible doesn't tell us

exactly what words Philip used. What do you think he might have said? *(Response)*

Suddenly the man said, "Look, here is some water. Couldn't I be baptized?"

(Baptism 57)
Philip answered, "If you believe with all your heart, you may."

The man said, "I believe that Jesus Christ is the Son of God" (Acts 8:37, KJV). Then he commanded the servant to stop the chariot so Philip and he could get down. They both went down into the water and Philip baptized him *(remove 54B, 56; add 57)*.

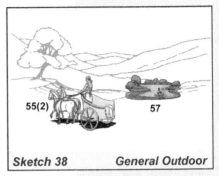

Sketch 38 *General Outdoor*

Being baptized did not save this man from his sin, any more than being baptized will save you or me from our sin. Being baptized showed his servants and the other people around him that something special had happened in his life. He had trusted Jesus to take away his sin and he now belonged to the family of God.

As they came up out of the water, the Holy Spirit suddenly took Philip away *(remove 57)* to another place where he preached the gospel to other people.

What did the Ethiopian man do? Look in verse 39 to find out. *(Have the teacher or a child read the verse aloud.)* Yes, though he didn't see Philip again, he went on his way home rejoicing! *(Add 56 to 55[2].)* He was happy and full of joy because he had obeyed God's Word by believing on the Lord Jesus Christ as his Savior from sin.

This Ethiopian man was now part of the Church (all those people who have trusted Jesus as Savior) and could tell others in Africa the good news about Jesus' death and resurrection. Many more people would come to believe in Jesus Christ as the Son of God and their Savior because Philip had been obedient to God's Word when he heard it.

Conclusion

Summary

(Believers 5, 25, Samaritans 17, Philip 81, chariot & driver 55[2], Ethiopian 56)

We have learned about several people who listened to God's Word and obeyed it. Who were they and how did they obey? *(Have the children name the people and tell how they obeyed as you or the children place the figures on the board.)*

- The believers *(place 5, 25 on the board)* obeyed part of Jesus' command and witnessed about Jesus in Jerusalem.
- The Samaritans *(add 17)* welcomed Philip and the Word of God.
- Philip *(add 81)* obeyed God and went to the desert road to Gaza.

Note (3)

In any translation other than the KJV, there is no verse 37 in chapter 8 because verse 37 does not appear in the earliest Greek manuscripts. It may have been a marginal commentary that later was included (before verses were numbered) to bridge between verses 36 and 38.

Note (4)

Isaiah's prophecy in chapter 53 is one of the most pointed presentations of the purpose for the death of the Messiah, Jesus Christ, in the entire Old Testament. God must have directed the Ethiopian to read this exact text as Philip came along!

Sketch 39 *Plain Background*

The Ethiopian man *(add 55[2], 56)* obeyed by believing in Jesus for forgiveness of sin and being baptized as a testimony of his faith.

Let's read Acts 8:8, 39 aloud together. *(Do so.)* How did the Samaritans and the Ethiopian man feel when they obeyed God's Word? Yes, they were full of joy.

What wonderful thing happened because Philip obeyed God's Word to him even though he didn't understand? Yes, the Ethiopian man believed in Jesus and took the message of Jesus back to his own country.

Application

("God's Word" chart from Introduction)

What does God want you to do when you hear his Word? *(Allow for response throughout.)* That's right; he wants us to obey, even when we don't understand or what he asks is not easy to do. What does God promise to do for us if we obey? He will bless us and give us the power to obey.

Earlier we looked at some verses and wrote down some things God wants us to do. *(Display the "God's Word" chart.)* Now let's think about the third column on our chart: "I need to obey." Is there something on this list that you know God wants you to obey but you find really hard to do? Something you need help with? Or maybe it's not on our list but is something you know God wants you to do? If that is true, then God is speaking to you to let you know he wants you to obey.

Response Activity

Distribute the **"God's Word" handouts** and pencils. ▲**#6** Have the children look at the first three lines and place a check mark in the "I Need to Obey" column next to any of those they know God wants them to obey.

Encourage any who want to obey God's Word by accepting Jesus as Savior to talk with you after class.

Have the children take their charts home. Tell them to read one of the verses each day, print what God says and then make a check mark if they need to obey. Be careful to remind them to ask for God's help to do what his Word has told them. **(5)**

Have the children bow their heads for a moment for silent prayer. Encourage them to ask God to help them during the coming week to obey in the areas they have checked. Invite any who wish to pray aloud. Then close in prayer, praying for them.

✍ TAKE HOME ITEMS

Distribute **memory verse tokens for Luke 11:28** and **Bible Study Helps for Lesson 7.**

▲ **Option #6**

For younger children, make handouts using only the two or three verses you printed on newsprint for the Introduction. Include the words of the verses as well as the references. Have them choose one of the three to work on obeying this week.

Note (5)

Bible Study Helps correlated with this series and designed to encourage daily Bible reading through the Book of Acts is available on the Resource CD. See pages xii and 148 for more information.

Saul Becomes a New Man
Theme: New Life

Lesson 8

✻ BEFORE YOU BEGIN...

Change!! We experience it daily in our lives, our families, our world. Change is rarely easy and it is not always desirable, but it is inevitable. So it is when we turn our lives over to Jesus Christ. The Holy Spirit living in us immediately begins to work toward change, to make us "new creatures." Not only for eternity, but in the "here and now." His changes are always for the good—to make us like the Lord Jesus. Sometimes these changes are dramatic; other times they are gradual.

The changes in Saul were dramatic! One day he was imprisoning Christians; a few days later he was preaching about the very Savior he had hated! The transformation itself must have been a tremendous witness to God's powerful working in the life of one who believed in the risen, living Savior! Help your children understand that if they have trusted Jesus Christ as their Savior, God can make changes in them, too. Use this lesson to help them focus on things in their lives that need changing—thoughts, attitudes or actions—and challenge them to trust Jesus as Savior and then allow him to work powerfully in their lives as well. *"Therefore, if anyone is in Christ, he is a new creation; old things have passed away; behold, all things have become new" (2 Corinthians 5:17, NKJV).*

AIM:

That the children may

- Know that God can change their lives for the better and make them new when they trust Jesus Christ as Savior.
- Respond by accepting Jesus as Savior and allowing God to begin to change the way they think and act.

📖 SCRIPTURE: Acts 8:1-3; Acts 9:1-22; 22:1-16; Galatians 1:13-24

♥ MEMORY VERSE: 2 Corinthians 5:17

Therefore if any man be in Christ, he is a new creature: old things are passed away; behold all things are become new. (KJV)

Therefore, if anyone is in Christ, he is a new creation; the old has gone, the new has come! (NIV)

59

▲ Option #1

Review game, Lessons 1-7: Before class, assign children in pairs or teams to each of the first seven lessons. Have them compose questions for reviewing that lesson.
In class, give each group opportunity to ask their questions. Have the class play against the teacher. Or, have them play against the clock, allowing so many seconds to answer each question.

▲ Option #2

For younger children: Shorten the memory verse to "If any man be in Christ, he is a new creature."

▲ Option #3

To illustrate, hold a coin in your fist. Explain that when we believe in Jesus as our Savior, it is as though he closes his hand around us and holds us tight—we are "in Christ." Cover that fist with your other hand and have a child try to get the coin. In Jesus, we are also in God's hand and Jesus said nothing can ever take us from it (John 10:28-29).

📁 MATERIALS TO GATHER

Memory verse visual for 2 Corinthians 5:17
Backgrounds: Review Chart, Plain Background, Courtyard, Council Room/Temple, General Outdoor, Plain Interior
Figures: 1R, R1-R8, 5, 10, 12, 17, 18, 19, 20, 21, 22, 23, 30, 31, 32B, 33, 34, 53, 59, 60, 71, 80, 84
Token holders & memory verse tokens for 2 Corinthians 5:17
Bible Study Helps for Lesson 8
Special:
- *For Introduction:* Pictures or mounted samples of caterpillars, butterflies, and cocoons
- *For Bible Content:* A 5" x 11" flannel or felt light ray
- *For Summary:* Word strips THOUGHTS, FEELINGS, ACTIONS
- *For Response Activity:* "Butterfly" handouts, pencils
- *For Options:* Materials for any options you choose to use
- *Note: Follow the instructions on page xii to prepare the light ray (pattern P-15 on page 146) to approximately 5" x 11", word strips, and the "Butterfly" handouts (pattern P-13 on page 145).*

🏠 REVIEW CHART

Display the Review Chart with 1R in place. Scatter R1-R7 pieces in random order on one side of the board. Have children one by one choose a symbol, give its theme and place it on the board as the class repeats the accompanying verse. Have R8 ready to use as indicated. Review Lesson 7 with the following True or False questions. Have the children give the correct answer for each false statement. ▲#1

TRUE or FALSE?

1. The believers had to move out of Jerusalem because they were being persecuted. *(True)*
2. God used Philip to do great miracles in Samaria and many people believed in Jesus. *(True)*
3. Philip decided to go to Gaza because he had friends there. *(False; he went because the Holy Spirit told him to go.)*
4. The Ethiopian was a man from Africa who had come to worship God in Jerusalem. *(True)*
5. The Ethiopian was searching for Philip in the desert. *(False; he was traveling home to Africa in his chariot.)*
6. Philip saw the Ethiopian reading from the Old Testament. *(True)*
7. Philip explained the Scriptures and the Ethiopian trusted in Jesus and was baptized. *(True)*

How many of you like to receive something new? Who has received something new recently and would like to tell us about it? *(Response)*

We all enjoy getting a new toy or game. But what happens to some of the old things we have? Yes, many times we need to get rid of them to make room for the new things.

Do you know that God does something like that in our lives? Today's building block for our Life House is *New Life (add R8 to the Chart)*. It can remind us of how God gets rid of the old sinful things in our lives and replaces them with something brand new—a new life—when we trust Jesus as our Savior. Our memory verse and Bible lesson will help us understand how this can happen.

♥ MEMORY VERSE

Use the visual to teach 2 Corinthians 5:17. ▲#2
Display the reference and the first three visual pieces and read them aloud in unison.

What words describe someone who has accepted the Lord Jesus as their Savior. *(Allow for response.)* Yes, the words are "in Christ" and a "new creature/creation." That sounds strange to us. Let's see what it means.

To be "in Christ" means to belong to God and be part of his family because you have accepted Jesus as your Savior. When you have done that, you are a child of God and nothing can ever change that. You belong to him forever! ▲#3

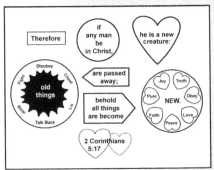

Being "in Christ" also means that God has given you a fresh start in this life as his child. He has forgiven your sin and given you his very own life—God the Holy Spirit living in you! Now you have God's power to help you be a "new creature" or "creation." God promises to help us live in a new way with new thoughts and new actions that please him.

This part of the verse *(display the last four visual pieces)* tells us what happens when God starts to make us a "new creation." Let's read it aloud together.

What "old things" in our lives will pass away or be removed? *(Response)* God has the power to help us get rid of—or "put off"— many sinful things we do and say like cheating, being unkind to others, having angry thoughts about another person, lying or fighting. Then he will help us replace them with—or "put on"—"new things," new ways of thinking and acting. Let's think of what some of these "new things" might be. *(Response)* That's right; truthfulness, honesty, obedience, kindness, helpfulness are some of the new things. ▲#4

This change doesn't happen all at once. It may take longer for some than for others. We must want to change and be made new. As we say yes to God and allow him to change us, others will notice a difference in us. Maybe they will wonder what is happening and then we can tell them that it is God who has made the changes in our lives. *(Work on memorizing the verse.)* ▲#5 ▲#6

▲ Option #4

1. To visualize your discussion of "old" and "new" things, print two headings—OLD & NEW— on newsprint or chalkboard. List "old" ways, as they are mentioned, under OLD. After each one, have the children look in their Bibles to see what "new" thing God says we should "put on" instead and write it under NEW. For example: for lying, Proverbs 8:7; for stealing, Ephesians 4:28; for unforgiveness and unkindness, Ephesians 4:32; for a bad attitude, Philippians 2:5 and Romans 12:2; for disobedience, Acts 5:29, Ephesians 6:1, Hebrews 13:7.

2. To help the children grasp "putting off" and "putting on," bring to class a set of old and new shirts. Pin a sign for "lying" (or other "old" things) to the old shirt and a sign for "truth" (or other "new" things) to the new shirt.

Have a child put on the old shirt. Discuss how God helps us to "put off" lying (have him take the shirt off) and "put on" truth (have him put on the new shirt) and how our "putting on" the new things pleases God.

▲ Option #5

Memorizing the verse: Mix the visual pieces on a table. Have the children each take a piece and place it on the board in its proper place in the verse. Every time a piece is added, have a different child say the verse.

When all pieces are on the board, divide the class and have them recite the verse back and forth—half the class saying the first word; the other half, the second word, and so on. Then remove the pieces and have them say it without visuals.

▲ Option #6

Give the children paper and crayon or pencil. Have them write the memory verse across the top of the paper, then draw an "old way" and a "new way" of living to illustrate the verse.

▲ Option #7

For younger children: Simplify Bible Content 1 by explaining that Saul studied the Old Testament and didn't believe that Jesus was the Son of God.

📖 BIBLE LESSON OUTLINE

Saul Becomes a New Man

■ Introduction

Looking for a change?

■ Bible Content

1. Saul persecutes the Church.
2. Saul meets Jesus on the Damascus road.
3. Ananias prays for Saul.
4. Saul begins to serve the Lord.

■ Conclusion

Summary

Application

Changing old ways of thinking and acting to new ways that please God

Response activity

Allowing God to help them change their ways of thinking and acting

📖 BIBLE LESSON

■ Introduction

Looking for a change?

Have pictures or mounted samples of a butterfly, a cocoon and a caterpillar ready.

Have you ever watched a butterfly flit from flower to flower? *(Allow for response throughout.)* Did you notice its beautiful coloring and how easily it moved? *(Show pictures or samples of butterfly.)* Who knows what the butterfly was before it could fly? Yes, it was a caterpillar *(show a sample or a picture of a caterpillar).*

Does the caterpillar look or act anything like the butterfly? Not at all! They are very different. How are they different? Caterpillars look like worms and can only crawl. Most are not beautiful to look at. But butterflies are beautifully-colored and fly easily from flower to flower.

How in the world did such a change occur? The caterpillar spun a cocoon and after so many days came out a new creature—the butterfly! It seems like a miracle, but God made it to change that way.

Do you know that God can change us to be very different from the way we are right now? In our lesson today we will meet a man whose whole way of life changed when he met Jesus! Listen carefully to see how God changed him.

Bible Content

1. **Saul persecutes the church.**
   (Acts 22:1-5; Galatians 1:13, 14;
   Acts 8:1-3; 9:1, 2) ▲#7

*(Pharisees 30, 33, 34, Saul 53, Gamaliel 31)
Place all the figures on the board.*
The Pharisees and other Jewish leaders were determined to stop the apostles from teaching about Jesus. They worked hard to keep all the laws they had added to God's laws, but in God's eyes they were very sinful because they pretended to be good when their hearts were filled with sinful thoughts and attitudes. Jesus once said they were like people who washed the outside of a cup but left the inside dirty. ▲#8

Sketch 40   Courtyard

This made the Pharisees very angry. They hated Jesus so much that they finally had him arrested and put to death on the cross. But Jesus rose from the dead and went back to heaven, and his followers kept on teaching about him. Now that Jesus was gone, the Pharisees persecuted the Church.

A young Pharisee named Saul *(indicate 53)* became a leader in this persecution. He was born in Tarsus, a large city far from Jerusalem, where he grew up with his parents, who were strict Jews. He learned from his father the trade of tent-making. When he was old enough, his parents sent him to Jerusalem to study the Old Testament Scriptures and laws.

Saul was a good student. He studied under Gamaliel *(indicate 31)*, one of the finest teachers of his day, and soon became an expert in Old Testament Scriptures and laws as well as a leader among the Jews.

Saul believed, as all Jews did, that someday the Messiah—a leader sent from God—would come, but he did not believe that Jesus was the Messiah. He thought Jesus was only a man—and not a very good one, because he claimed to be God, and everyone knew no man could be God. Saul thought the disciples were talking against God and against God's laws because they taught that Jesus was the Son of God. This made him more determined than ever that all the apostles should be put to death as Stephen had been. So, when Saul went from house to house in Jerusalem, arresting men and women who believed in Jesus and dragging them off to prison, he thought he was pleasing God.

▲ Option #8

Take to class a pretty cup or mug that is shiny clean on the outside, but dirtied with charcoal or even mud on the inside. Hold the cup up to be admired by the class. Then allow the children to look at the inside and ask if they would want to drink from that cup. Help them understand that sinful thoughts and attitudes in our hearts are as repulsive to God as the dirty inside of the cup is to us.

(Saul 84, High Priest 33)
Saul *(place 84 on the board)* was furious when he heard that the believers were teaching the good news about Jesus' death and resurrection wherever they went after they left Jerusalem. They must be stopped! So one day he went to the high priest, the religious leader of the Jews *(add 33)*, and asked him for letters to the synagogues in Damascus giving him authority to arrest any believers in that city and bring them back to Jerusalem to be punished.

Sketch 41   Council Room/ Temple

The high priest gladly wrote the letters, telling the Jewish leaders in Damascus what Saul was coming to do. It wasn't long until all the believers in Damascus had heard that Saul was on his way! How do you think they felt?

2. Saul meets Jesus on the Damascus road.
(Acts 9:3-9; 22:6-11)

Sketch 42 — General Outdoor

(Saul 53, soldier 32B, men 60)
Damascus was a large city about ten days travel from Jerusalem. Saul and his companions *(place all the figures on the board)* probably walked or rode donkeys on that long trip. ▲#9 At noontime of the last day they were very near the city. The sun was hot and bright. They were probably thirsty and looking forward to the end of their trip when a very startling thing happened! *(Leave all the figures on the board.)*

Sketch 43 — General Outdoor

(Flannel or felt light ray; Saul 59)
Suddenly a bright light from heaven flashed down on Saul *(add light ray)*. It was brighter than the noonday sun! Saul fell to the ground in fear *(remove 53; add 59)*. He heard a voice calling his name, "Saul! Saul! Why are you persecuting me?"

"Who are you?" Saul asked.

"I am Jesus of Nazareth whom you are persecuting," he answered.

"What do you want me to do, Lord?" Saul questioned.

"Get up and go into the city. There you will be told what you are to do," was the Lord's answer.

The men traveling with Saul were astonished and couldn't think of a thing to say! They saw the light and heard the sound of a voice, but were not able to understand the words. And they couldn't see anyone!

When Saul got to his feet he couldn't see. The bright light had blinded him. His friends took him by the hand and led him into Damascus.

3. Ananias prays for Saul.
(Acts 9:10-18; 22:12-16)

Sketch 44 — Plain Interior

(Saul 12, Ananias 5, 84)
Saul *(place 12 on the board)* was blind for three days. All that time he did not eat or drink anything. What do you think Saul was doing? *(Response)* Yes, I imagine that he was thinking about Jesus. He finally realized he had been wrong! Jesus really was the Son of God who had died for him! Jesus was the Messiah, the one for whom the Jews had waited so long!

Saul must have felt terrible when he thought about how he had persecuted Jesus' followers. He had thought he was pleasing God. Now he realized he had actually been sinning against God.

Many disciples of the Lord Jesus lived in the city of Damascus. One was named Ananias *(hold up 5 in your hand)*. One day God called him by name: "Ananias." ◿(1)

Ananias knew the voice of the Lord, and he answered at once, "Yes, Lord."

The Lord said, "Go to the home of Judas who lives on Straight Street and ask for a man from Tarsus named Saul. He is praying, and I have told him that a man named Ananias will come and put his hands on him so he can see again."

Ananias was very surprised. "Lord," he said, "I have heard of this man Saul and how he has harmed the believers in Jerusalem. Now he's come here with permission from the high priest to arrest anyone who believes in Jesus."

The Lord replied, "Don't be afraid to go. I have chosen this man to be my witness to the Gentiles and to the Jews. He will stand before kings and witness for me. He will suffer much for my name."

Then Ananias *(add 5)* went to Judas' house and found Saul. He placed his hands on him and said, "Brother Saul, the Lord Jesus who appeared to you on your way here has sent me so that you can see again and be filled with the Holy Spirit." Immediately Saul was able to see again. Then he *(remove 12; add 84)* got up and was baptized to show that he was now a believer in the Lord Jesus. *(Remove 5; leave 84 on the board.)*

4. Saul begins to serve the Lord.
   (Acts 9:19-22; Galatians 1:15-24)

At some point after the Lord Jesus appeared to Saul and talked with him, Saul recognized that Jesus truly was the Son of God. At that moment Saul was forgiven of his sin and became part of God's family. He was changed from hating the Lord Jesus to loving him and wanting to serve him. The Holy Spirit came to live in him and began making him like the Lord Jesus.

God told Saul that He had a special work for him to do. He was to go and tell the world, both Jews and Gentiles, that Jesus is the Son of God—and he would be persecuted for doing it!

(Crowd 17, Jews 30 31, man 80, Saul 53)
Place 17, 30, 31, 80 on the board.

Saul was eager to obey the Lord. Right away *(add 53)* he went to the synagogues in Damascus and preached that Jesus is the Son of God.

The people who heard him were amazed. "Isn't this Saul who was persecuting everybody who believed in Jesus?" they said to each other. "Didn't he come here to arrest all the believers and take them back to Jerusalem as prisoners? What has happened to him?" Some listened to what he had to say, but some got very angry and wanted to kill him.

▲ **Option #9**

Use a map to show the distance between Jerusalem and Damascus (in Syria). Also, use an example of a similar point-to-point distance your children would understand (about 65 miles).

◿ **Note (1)**

The word *vision* was left out of the story account (Acts 9:10-14). If you choose to use it or have your chldren read from the text, be ready to explain the word. Seeing a vision is seeing something that has not yet happened or is not visible without God's help; that is, God enabled Saul to see Ananias coming to restore his sight. And Ananias was not sleeping at the time God spoke to him in a vision, so his vision was not a dream.

Sketch 45   Courtyard

Saul had not been with the apostles during the three years when the Lord Jesus was their teacher on earth. He knew that he needed to know the Lord Jesus much better, so he went off by himself to Arabia for three years. There he had time to pray and study God's Word.

■ Conclusion

Summary

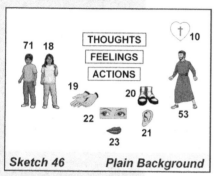

Sketch 46   Plain Background

(Saul 53, heart 10, eyes 22, ears 21, lips 23, hands 19, feet 20; word strips THOUGHTS, FEELINGS, ACTIONS)

When Saul *(place 53 on the board)* believed *(add 10)* in Jesus as his Savior, God began to make changes in his life. Let's look at some of the things in Saul's life which were made new.

How did Saul's thoughts change? *(Allow for response throughout; add THOUGHTS.)* What did he think about Jesus before he met him on the road? Yes, he was a liar and an imposter. What did he think about Jesus afterward? Yes, he truly is the Son of God. God changed Saul's thinking.

How did his feelings *(add FEELINGS)* change about the Lord Jesus and those who believed *(indicate 10)* in him? Yes, instead of feeling anger and hatred toward them, he loved them and was sorry for hurting them.

How did Saul's actions *(add ACTIONS)* change? *(Add 22, 21, 23, 19, 20. Allow the children to choose one and tell how Saul changed in that area.)* He studied God's Word *(eye)* and listened to God *(ear)*. Instead of angrily making false accusations against the believers *(mouth)*, he talked about Jesus to all who would listen. He no longer used his hands and feet to punish the believers and take them to prison. Instead he served God by going to places that didn't know about Jesus and teaching them. God the Holy Spirit was living in Saul and changing him into a "new creature."

Application

(Girl 18, boy 71)

Do you know that God can change you and me *(add 18, 71)* just as he changed Saul? He can if we are "in Christ." Who remembers what it means to be "in Christ"? *(Response)* Yes, to belong to God's family by accepting Jesus as Savior. That is the first step toward being a "new creature." If you have never done that, you may do it today. Come after class to talk with me about it.

If you are "in Christ" as Saul was, then you, too, have God the Holy Spirit living in you. He is the one who can help you change—"put off"—your old sinful habits and "put on" new ways of living that please him. *(Use figures 10, 19, 20, 21, 22, 23 on the board to discuss with the children how they can "put off" sinful habits and then "put on" new ways to replace them. For example, Lips: grumbling when asked to do* chores for Mom vs. saying, "Sure, I'll help!"; Heart: feeling hurt because another made the team when you didn't vs. being happy for that person; Eyes: reading or looking at books, videos or TV programs you know are wrong and sinful vs. using your eyes to read or see only those things that please God, and so on.)   ▲#10

As we've been talking about these things, have you thought of something in your life that needs to be changed from the "old" to the "new"? Perhaps the words you say or the things you look at or some feelings in your heart or where you let your feet take you or how you use your hands? The Lord Jesus cares about every part of your life and wants to help you change old habits to new ways of living. Think about that as we say our verse together. *(Do so.)*

Let's talk to the Lord Jesus now. Ask him to give you his power to "put off" this "old thing" and help you "put on" a "new thing" so that you can begin to think and act in a new way will please him.

Response Activity

Invite any who have not yet trusted Jesus Christ as Savior to do that today so that they will be "in Christ."

Have all children bow their heads. Encourage those who know they are "in Christ" to pray silently, telling the Lord Jesus they want to be changed and are willing to give up the "old" sinful way they are thinking of (have them name it specifically in their prayer) and have it replaced with a "new" way. Distribute the **"Butterfly" handouts** *and pencils. Have the children print the "old" habit on the caterpillar and the "new" way on the butterfly, then take them home as reminders to ask for God's help to put off old ways and put on the new.*

✍ TAKE HOME ITEMS

Distribute **memory verse tokens for 2 Corinthians 5:17 and Bible Study Helps for Lesson 8.**

▲ **Option #10**

Review the "put off" / "put on" concept using the shirt object lesson from the memory verse explanation.

Dorcas Is Raised from the Dead
Theme: Love

Lesson 9

❋ BEFORE YOU BEGIN...

Everyone longs to be loved unconditionally—but who will do the loving? People who will accept others and love them with "no strings attached" are desperately needed in a world and culture that is primarily me-oriented! Children are being taught that they have "rights" and must think of themselves first. Individuals are often so self-involved that they are unable to see beyond their own circle. Many are unwilling to go the extra mile for others. Believers who are willing to love with Christ's love can have tremendous impact on the world around them.

This Scripture passage illustrates that truth. Without thought of reward, Peter and Dorcas—each in their own sphere—exemplify selfless love, first for God and then for others. Use the lesson to help your children grasp how important it is to not just say they love God and belong to him, but to also show their love by their actions, their words and their attitudes toward others. Help them begin to plan regularly how they will demonstrate God's love to the people around them, even those who aren't easy to love. *"But God demonstrates His own love toward us, in that while we were still sinners, Christ died for us" (Romans 5:8, NJKV).*

☞ AIM:

That the children may

- Know that God wants us to show our love for him by the way we treat others.

- Respond by showing God's love to someone this week.

📖 SCRIPTURE: Acts 9:32-42

♥ MEMORY VERSE: 1 Peter 1:22

See that ye love one another with a pure heart fervently. (KJV)
Love one another deeply, from the heart. (NIV)

MATERIALS TO GATHER

Memory verse visual for 1 Peter 1:22
Backgrounds: Review Chart, Plain Background, General Interior, Plain Interior
Figures: 1R, R1-R9, 1, 6A, 11, 14, 24, 25, 39, 44, 63A, 63B, 64A, 64B, 65A, 65B, 66
Token holders & memory verse tokens for 1 Peter 1:22
Bible Study Helps for Lesson 9
Special:
- **For Bible Content:** MAP OF ISRAEL from Lesson 7
- **For Application:** Newsprint & marker or chalkboard & chalk
- **For Response Activity:** "Heart" handouts, pencils
- **For Options:** Materials for any options you choose to use
- **Note:** Follow the instructions on page xii to prepare the "Heart" handouts (pattern P-14 on page 145).

 REVIEW CHART

Display the Review Chart with 1 R and R1-R7 in place. Add R8 as you review, using the following questions. Have R9 ready to use when indicated.

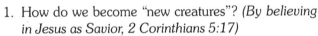

1. How do we become "new creatures"? *(By believing in Jesus as Savior, 2 Corinthians 5:17)*
2. What does it mean to be "in Christ"? *(To belong to God's family and to live for him)*
3. What are some of the "new things" God wants to build into our lives? *(Obedience, truthfulness, love)*
4. How did Saul become a changed or new person? *(He received Christ as Savior.)*
5. How did Saul's life change after he became a believer in Jesus? *(He preached about the Lord Jesus rather than speaking against him and persecuting the Christians.)*

Today we add *Love* to our Life House *(add R9)*. It is a very important building block for our lives. When Jesus was on earth, He often spoke to his disciples about loving one another. Our lesson and memory verse will help us understand what this word really means and how God wants us to show love to others.

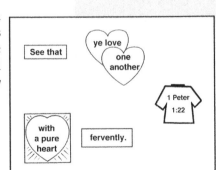

 MEMORY VERSE

Use the visual to teach 1 Peter 1:22 as part of Bible Content 1.

📖 BIBLE LESSON OUTLINE

Dorcas Is Raised from the Dead

■ Introduction

How do we know people love us?

■ Bible Content

1. Peter teaches us to love others.
    Memory verse presentation
2. Peter shows love by healing Aeneas.
3. Peter shows love by raising Dorcas from the dead.

■ Conclusion

Summary

Application
   Thinking of ways to show love to others

Response Activity
   Showing love to someone this week

📖 BIBLE LESSON

■ Introduction

How do we know people love us?

How do you know if people love you? *(Encourage response throughout.)* Yes, by what they say to you and the things they do for you. How do other people know that you love them? Is it enough to just say, I love you? Will your mother think you love her if you fuss and grumble every time she asks you to do something? No, saying the words isn't enough. How you respond when she asks you to do something shows whether you really love her or not. ▲#1

How do we know that Jesus loves us? Yes, we know because of what he says in the Bible (John 3:16) and because he died for us on the cross. How can we show our love for the Lord Jesus? *(Let children respond.)* Jesus once said to his disciples, If you love me, you will do what I say (John 14:15). So we show our love for him by obeying his commands. He also said, You should love each other like I have loved you (John 15:12). We show we love him by doing loving things for others.

▲ **Option #1**

Divide class into small groups to prepare a short skit on how they would show love or respond in a loving way in the following situations:

1. Your mom asks you to watch your little brother during your practice ball game.
2. Your teacher asks you to help a classmate with an assignment—someone who is always teasing and making fun of you.
3. You notice that a new student in your class is always alone, at lunch time and recess.
4. Some children in your neighborhood have only a dad at home. They never seem to have good lunches at school or warm clothes in winter and they have very few toys to play with.

The children could also suggest their own ideas for situations.

Bible Content

1. Peter teaches us to love others.
Memory verse presentation

Use the visual to teach 1 Peter 1:22 when indicated.
Peter wrote about loving others in one of his letters to believers who were being persecuted. Let's find Peter's letters in our Bibles. They are toward the end of the New Testament and are called 1 Peter and 2 Peter. *(Help any who are unfamiliar with their Bibles.)* Our memory verse is in 1 Peter *(display the visual and have the class read the verse together)*.

Peter was writing to people who believed in Jesus. We live many years later, but this verse is written to all of us who have received Jesus as Savior.

What word tells us *how* we are to love each other? Yes, it's *fervently (deeply)*. To love others *fervently (deeply)* is to love them enthusiastically and with the right motives.

If we are helpful or kind to someone in order to get something from them in return, we are really being selfish and only pretending to love them. But if we are helpful and kind to others because we love Jesus and want them to love him too, we are showing real love to them. It is not easy to love people this way, but God the Holy Spirit living in us can help us do it, even when they say or do things we don't like. *(Work on memorizing the verse.)* ▲#2

2. Peter shows love by healing Aeneas.
(Acts 9:32-35)

▲ **Option #2**

Memorizing the verse: Print the complete verse and reference on several sheets of different-colored construction paper. Cut each sheet into several pieces and hide them around the room before class.

Divide class into as many groups as you have colored sheets and assign a color to each group. At a signal, have them look for their colored pieces (being careful not to touch other colors), put them together to complete the puzzle and then compete to see which group can say the verse correctly.

(Peter 11, Aeneas 63A, 24, bed 63B.)
Today we are going to see how Peter and some of the other early believers showed their love for Jesus by the way they treated others. You remember that when Saul began to persecute the church in Jerusalem, the believers scattered, looking for safe places to live. Wherever they went they told the good news about Jesus. Many people believed their message and began to meet with them.

Peter and the other apostles were still living in Jerusalem, but Peter spent much of his time traveling from place to place, teaching the Word of God to the new believers. Peter loved Jesus and he wanted others to know about him.

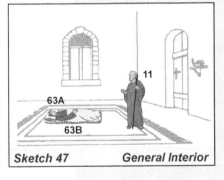

Sketch 47   *General Interior*

One time Peter *(place 11 on the board)* went to visit the believers in a small town called Lydda. There he met a man named Aeneas *(add 63A, 63B)* who had been paralyzed (unable to walk) for eight years. No one had been able to help him. Peter must have wanted Aeneas and his friends to know how much God loved them. He knew that he could tell them about God's love, but they needed to see love in a practical way. Peter said, "Aeneas, Jesus Christ heals you. Get up and make your bed" *(remove 63A; add 24)*. Immediately Aeneas stood up. He was healed! Everyone from Lydda and even nearby villages came to see the paralyzed man who now was able to walk! When they saw what God's wonderful power had done, they all believed in the Lord.

3. Peter shows love by raising Dorcas from the dead. (Acts 9:36-42)

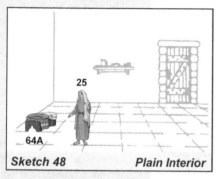

Sketch 48 — Plain Interior

(MAP OF ISRAEL; Dorcas 25, stool 64A)
Joppa was a seaport town about ten miles from Lydda *(indicate cities on the map)*. Many ships sailed in and out of its harbor bringing people from all over the world.

A group of believers met together there to worship the Lord. One of these believers was a woman named Dorcas *(place 25 on the board)*, who was always doing something to help others or care for the poor. She spent many hours sewing, making robes *(add 64A)* and other clothing for the needy. Dorcas was known all over the city because of her love for others and her work for them.

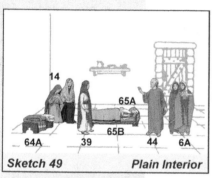

Sketch 49 — Plain Interior

(Women 6A, 14, 39, Dorcas 65A, bed 65B, Peter 44, arm 64B)
While Peter was in Lydda, Dorcas became sick and died *(remove 25)*. Friends *(add 6A)* washed her body and laid it in an upstairs room *(add 65A, 65B)*. All the believers were sad and crying *(add 14, 39)*. When they heard that Peter was in Lydda, they said to each other, "Let's send for him!"

Two men went quickly, found Peter and urged him, "Come with us right away!"

Peter didn't hesitate. He and the two men immediately started back to Joppa. When they arrived, Peter *(add 44)* was taken to the room where Dorcas' body lay. All around him people were crying.

"See," said a mother, "here is the clothing *(add 64B to 39)* she made for my children last year."

"She came to help us when my husband died," said another, "and she made warm clothing for us."

Peter looked at all the people who loved Dorcas and thought about how kind she had been to them. She had demonstrated her love for God by the way she treated people. Peter asked Dorcas' friends to leave the room. *(Remove 6A, 14, 39, 64B.)* After they had gone, Peter got down on his knees and prayed. He knew that he had no power to help this woman, but he also knew that God's power could do anything. He wanted to show the love of God to these people. *(Leave all the figures on the board.)*

(Peter 15, Dorcas 66, 25)

After Peter *(remove 44; add 15)* prayed, he turned toward the dead woman and said, "Dorcas, get up!"

Dorcas opened her eyes just as if she were waking up out of a sleep. When she saw Peter, she *(remove 65A; add 66)* sat up. He took her by the hand and helped her stand *(remove 66; add 25)*. Then he opened the door and called to her friends who were waiting outside. How happy they must have been when they saw her alive!

Word of this miracle spread all through the city of Joppa. Many people believed in the Lord Jesus when they heard of his mighty power to raise Dorcas from the dead.

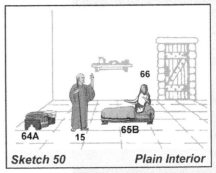

Sketch 50   **Plain Interior**

■ Conclusion

Summary

(Dorcas 25, Peter 15)

Let's say our memory verse together. *(Do so.)* Today we learned of some ways that Dorcas and Peter showed God's love to the people around them. How did Dorcas show her love for others? *(Place 25 on the board; encourage response throughout.)* Yes, she cared about people and used her time, her money and her ability to make clothes for the poor and help those who were in need. People loved her because they knew she loved them.

How did Peter *(add 15)* show love to others? He taught the Word of God to new believers. He took the time to visit Aeneas and heal him. He traveled to another town to help Dorcas, and God used him to bring her back to life. Peter showed his love for others by helping them, praying for them and telling them about Jesus.

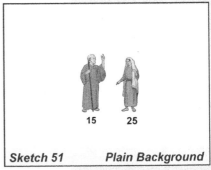

Sketch 51   **Plain Background**

Peter and Dorcas could do all these things for people, because they knew that God loved them, and they wanted to obey Jesus' command to love others. And God the Holy Spirit living in them helped them.

Peter and Dorcas showed their love by the words they spoke, the way they lived and the many kind acts they did for people. It wasn't always easy. Many people didn't want to hear about Jesus. But because Peter and Dorcas loved Jesus, they were able to help others and give to those who were in need.

What happened as a result of the miracles God did through Peter for Aeneas and Dorcas? Yes, God's power made them both well, but there was something more. Many people believed in Jesus because Peter had showed God's love.

Application

(Newsprint & markers or chalkboard & chalk)

What does our memory verse say we are to do? Yes, love each other with a pure heart fervently. Do you love others with that kind of love? We need God's help to do that. If you have never trusted Jesus as your Savior, you need to do that today. He is the One who gives us the love we need for others.

If you have already trusted Jesus, can you think of someone who needs you to show love to them? Maybe your mom or dad or one of your brothers or sisters? Or perhaps someone at school or in your neighborhood you do not like very much. Or someone who isn't always kind to you? Perhaps that person needs to see God's love in you. He may not even know Jesus as Savior.

What are some ways you could show love to that person? *(List responses on newsprint or chalkboard. If necessary, suggest an idea or two such as: helping brother or sister with chores; taking time to help a classmate with homework; offering to help parents without being asked; inviting someone to play a game with you.)*

Showing love to others is not always easy, but if we ask God to fill us with his love and help us to act in a loving way when we don't feel like it, he will do it. Then we will soon see how others are helped and how good we feel because people can see God's love in our lives. Perhaps some will even believe in Jesus because of us! ▲#3

▲ Option #3

Review the principle of "putting off" old ways and "putting on" new ways from Lesson 8. To illustrate, make two flashcards. Punch holes in them and attach string so they can be hung around a child's neck. On one print No love; on the other, God's love.

Hang the No love card around a child's neck. Then encourage the child to "put off" the No love card and "put on" God's love.

Response Activity

Distribute the **"Heart" handouts** and pencils. Guide the children to think of one person to whom they will show love this week and one specific way they will do it. Have them print the person's name on the heart along with what they plan to do. Tell them to take it home and put it where they will see it each day as a reminder of what they plan to do. Next week give them opportunity to tell how God helped them and what happened as a result. Pray with them, asking God to help them carry out their plan.

✍ TAKE HOME ITEMS

Distribute **memory verse tokens for 1 Peter 1:22** and **Bible Study Helps for Lesson 9**.

Peter Tells Cornelius the Gospel
Theme: Accepting Others

Lesson 10

  BEFORE YOU BEGIN...

Prejudice, racism and intolerance of personal differences create grave problems today. Children learn such attitudes early through example. Often we see them acting or reacting to others cruelly without understanding why they do it or what the consequences might be. It does not always involve race or skin color or limitations. It can be any small difference that makes one child seem different from the others. We must teach our children that we all are sinners, that "God so loved the world that he gave his only…Son," and that they should respect all people as those for whom Christ died. Everyone should hear the gospel because the risen Christ said, "Go into all the world … preach the gospel to every creature" (Mark 16:15).

Peter's ministry was limited by his prejudice against the Gentiles until God intervened to teach Peter his way of looking at things. Peter was never the same; God had changed his mindset and his heart attitude. Help your children see that God can change our hearts, too. He can help us accept others and show his love to them—no matter how different from us they may be. *"For I am not ashamed of the gospel of Christ, for it is the power of God to salvation for everyone who believes, for the Jew first and also for the Greek" (Romans 1:16, NKJV).*

AIM:

That the children may

- Know that God loves *all* people and wants them to hear the good news about Jesus.
- Respond by expressing God's love in word and action to people who are different from them so that they can be saved.

SCRIPTURE: Acts 9:43–10:48

MEMORY VERSE: Romans 3:22, 23

For there is no difference, for all have sinned, and come short of the glory of God. (KJV)

There is no difference, for all have sinned and fall short of the glory of God. (NIV)

▲ **Option #1**

Encourage children who arrive early to write review questions for previous lessons.

Allow those who do so to ask their questions to the rest of the class during review time.

📁 **MATERIALS TO GATHER**

Memory verse visual for Romans 3:22, 23
Backgrounds: Review Chart, Plain Background, General Interior, Roof Overlay, City Street
Figures: 1R, R1-R10, 6A, 6C, 6D, 6E, 7A, 11, 15, 17, 32A, 32B, 68, 69, 70, 73(2), 81
Token holders & memory verse tokens for Romans 3:22, 23
Bible Study Helps for Lesson 10
Special:
- *For Bible Content 2 & 3:* MAP OF ISRAEL from Lesson 7
- *For Application:* Newsprint & marker
- *For Response Activity:* "A Plan for Accepting Others" handouts, pencils
- *For Options:* Materials for any options you choose to use
- *Note:* Follow the instructions on page xii to prepare the "A Plan for Accepting Others" handouts (pattern P-7 on page 142).

🏠 **REVIEW CHART**

Display the Review Chart with 1R in place and R1-R9 in random order on the board. Have individuals choose a symbol and place it in its proper place as the class repeats its verse and theme. Have R10 ready to use when indicated. Use the following questions to review Lessons 1-9. ▲#1

1. What promise did the angels give the disciples after Jesus went back to heaven? *(That Jesus would return)*
2. Whom did God send to be with the believers after Jesus went back to heaven? *(The Holy Spirit)*
3. What miracle did God help Peter and John perform? *(Healing the lame man)*
4. What do we mean by the word salvation? *(Being saved from God's punishment for our sin by accepting Christ as Savior)*
5. What sin did Ananias and Sapphira commit? *(They lied to God.)*
6. What does the word obey mean? *(To listen to one who has authority over us and then do what we are told)*
7. Give an example of what it means to obey God rather than man. *(E.g., If a person tells you to do something that God does not want you to do, obey God and not the person.)*
8. What miracle did God do for Peter and John in prison? *(He sent an angel to free them.)*
9. Why did the Jewish leaders put Stephen to death? *(He taught that Jesus is the Son of God.)*
10. Who gave Stephen courage and joy when he was dying? *(God, the Holy Spirit)*

11. What happened because Philip obeyed God and went to the desert road to Gaza? *(The Ethiopian man trusted Christ as his Savior.)*
12. What changes took place in Saul's life when he met Christ on the road to Damascus? *(He stopped hurting the believers and began to tell everyone that Jesus is God's Son.)*
13. In what ways did Dorcas show God's love to others? *(She made clothes and gave to the poor.)*
14. What are some ways we can show love to other people?

The building block we add to our Life House today is called *Accepting Others (place R10 on the review chart).* **(1)** God wants us to accept other people. What do you think we mean by that? *(Encourage response.)* To accept others means to recognize that God made them special and that he loves and values them, no matter how they dress, what color their skin is, what language they speak or how they behave. If we could see all the members of the Church, God's big family on earth, they would look very different to us in the way they dress and the color of their skins. They would sound very different, too, for they speak many different languages. God accepts them all because they have received Jesus as their Savior and become part of God's family. He wants us to accept them, too.

God does not show favoritism. He sent Jesus to die for "the world" so that each individual could, if they would, receive him as Savior and have their sins forgiven. He wants us to see all people as those for whom Jesus died and express his love to them by our words and our behavior. Sometimes this is difficult, but God the Holy Spirit living in us will help us. When we show God's love to people who do not know him, they will pay more attention when we tell them the good news about Jesus and some will be saved. **(2)**

♥ MEMORY VERSE

Use the visual to teach Romans 3:22, 23 when indicated.

Our memory verse was written to help a group of believers in the early Church understand an important truth. *(Display the visual pieces for verse 22 and read the words aloud with the class).*

At this time most of the people who had believed in Jesus were Jews. They had been taught for hundreds of years that they were God's chosen people, so they thought God loved them more than he loved anyone else. They also had become proud about being God's chosen people. They thought they were better than anyone else and began to look down on anyone who wasn't a Jew. God used Paul, who wrote these words, to let them know that these thoughts and attitudes were not right. God says in this verse that there is no difference. The Jew has no right to consider himself superior to anyone else.

▲ Note (1)

1. Though words such as "accepting others" and "tolerance" are the subject of serious suspicion in some circles, they legitimately express godly characteristics when

(continued on page 78)

▲ Note (2)

At issue in this lesson is the question, Can we accept a person without agreeing with him? It is important for us to realize that when we do not accept someone, he (or she) may perceive that as an attack on his person rather than on his position or opinion. *Acceptance* is the opposite of *prejudice*. Racial prejudice is an attitude that says, *Your race is different from mine; therefore, it is inferior.* Prejudice can exist in other areas, such as **age:** *You're older; therefore, I am superior;* **ability:** *I can do this better than you; therefore, I am better than you;* **condition:** *You have a disability; therefore, you*

are inferior to me; **position:** *I have a better job or I live in a better neighborhood; therefore, you are inferior to me.*

(continued from page 77) understood properly. When we speak of accepting others in this lesson, we do not mean we are to accept their sinful ways nor the current notion that *anything goes, no one has the right to judge* and *there are no absolute standards for living.*

2. Rather, we mean accepting everyone as fellow members of the human race, created in the image of God, commonly corrupted by the fall, objects of God's love when he sent his Son Jesus and equally in need of hearing the gospel message.

The biblical concept of tolerance has often been twisted to the pluralistic notion that since there is no absolute truth, everyone's beliefs are equally valid and therefore must be tolerated. Not to do so is thought to be intolerant, which is then seen to be the greatest sin of all in today's world. As a teacher of God's truth you need to carefully lead your children to show respect toward those who are different from them. Only then will they have opportunity to share the gospel with them.

Romans 3:23 tells us why there is no difference. *(Display the visual pieces for verse 23 and read the words aloud together.)* What does it say about all of us? *(Response)* Yes, we all have sinned. Who can tell us what sin is? *(Response)* Sin is disobeying God and his Word in our actions, our words, our thoughts and our attitudes. What else does the verse say about us? We have come short of God's glory or of who God is. Because God is holy and we are sinners, we can never measure up to God's standard of perfection. ▲#2

The Jews had no right to think they were better than others and neither do we. No matter how good we think we are, how nice we look or dress, how rich or poor we are, how great we are at sports or music, how well we do at school, what the color of our skin is, or our family origin, we all have the same problem—we are sinners who have come short of God's glory. And we all have the same need—to hear the gospel so we can have the opportunity of believing in the Lord Jesus Christ. *(Work on memorizing the verse.)* ▲#3

📖 BIBLE LESSON OUTLINE

Peter Tells Cornelius the Gospel

▪ Introduction

Joey's problem

▪ Bible Content

1. God's plan for the Jews.
2. God's plan for the Gentiles.
3. Cornelius worships God.
4. Peter learns a lesson.
5. Peter teaches Cornelius and other Gentiles.

▪ Conclusion

Summary

Application
   Accepting those who are different from me

Response Activity
   Committing to accepting others

📖 BIBLE LESSON

▪ Introduction

Joey's problem

One of Joey's favorite experiences in school was playing ball during recess. He and several other boys had developed a close friendship so that they always chose each other to be on the same team. And, as it turned out, they usually won the choose-up games at recess.

When two new kids came into their class, Joey was faced with a problem. One day the teacher said, "Joey, I notice that the two new boys never get to play ball at recess. Why don't you choose them to be on your team so that the others will follow your example and include them in the game. Maybe it will help them get acquainted."

But those boys were so different! They had just moved from another country. Neither of them could speak nor understand much English, so they kept to themselves. And they didn't seem to know much about playing ball. Joey was afraid they would make his team lose.

When Joey told his friends what the teacher had suggested, they objected right away. "Why should we break up our group?" they said. "We might not win any more! We don't want those 'losers' on our team!"

Joey was miserable. He didn't like the new boys much either because they seemed so different and unfriendly. He knew they needed friends, but he wanted his friends to like him and he liked winning games. What made it even harder was that Joey had asked Jesus to be his Savior. He knew that God wanted him to show his love to the boys so he could tell them about Jesus. Joey had a big problem and wasn't sure how to solve it.

Today we will see that Peter once faced a similar problem and learn how God helped him. Listen to see if you can discover Peter's problem and God's answer.

Bible Content

1. God's plan for the Jews

(JEW 73, GENTILE 73)

There was a time when Peter did not understand that there is no difference with God, that he loved the Greeks and the Romans just as much as he did the Jews, and that anyone in the whole world could be accepted into God's family through trusting in the name of Jesus. God taught Peter this truth in a very wonderful way.

Hundreds of years before Peter and the other disciples lived, God called a man named Abraham to be the father of a chosen group of people we call Jews *(place JEW 73 on the board)* or the nation of Israel. The Old Testament tells their story.

God chose the Jewish people for a very special purpose. Through them he gave the world his Word, the Bible, and his Son Jesus (who had a Jewish mother). He wanted his chosen people to show the rest of the world what he was like by the way they lived and how they obeyed him and trusted him. Then other nations would want to love God and worship him instead of their idols.

▲ Option #2

To illustrate the concept of not measuring up, have a child stand next to you and try to stretch up to be as tall as you are. Or, ask a child to stretch a 12-inch ruler to match a yardstick. As the child cannot measure up to the teacher's height and the 12-inch ruler cannot measure up to the yardstick, so we who are sinners can never reach (or measure up to) God's standard of holiness by ourselves.

▲ Option #3

Memorizing the verse: Have the class emphasize different words each time they repeat the verse: *First time:* no, all, short, God; *Second time:* difference, sinned, short, God.

Have several children, one at a time, remove the visual pieces and place them on a table in random order. Each time have another child say the verse without the missing pieces. Continue until all

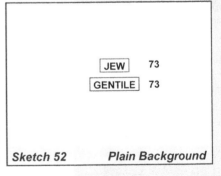

Sketch 52   Plain Background

pieces have been removed and the verse repeated several times. Finally, have children who have not had a turn display the visual pieces in correct order. Repeat the verse together again.

▲ **Option #4**

Before class, print Mark 16:15 or Matthew 28:19 on newsprint.

In class, display the verse and have the children read it aloud together to see Jesus' words to the disciples.

Or, have them find the verse in their Bibles and read it together.

▲ **Option #5**

Before class, draw on newsprint a simple map of Israel to be used on the floor (follow pattern P-1 on page 138); print place names (Jerusalem, Judea, Samaria, Joppa, Caesarea) on cards or construction paper.

In class, place the map on the floor and give the cards to children to place in the correct places on the map as they are mentioned. Or, punch holes in the cards and attach cord or ribbon so children can wear them and stand in the proper places on the map.

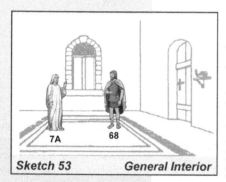

Sketch 53   General Interior

To help Israel be different from the other peoples on earth, God gave them special instructions or laws about how they should worship him, how they should live and even what foods they should eat. For example, they were allowed to eat the meat of cows and sheep (which God designated "clean" or acceptable), but they were never to eat pigs or camels (which God designated "unclean" or unacceptable).

Sadly, the Jews forgot that they were supposed to show the rest of the world what God was like. Instead, they came to believe that God loved only them, and they looked down on anyone who was not a Jew—they called them Gentiles *(add GENTILE 73)*—because they did not observe the Jewish laws.

The Jews who had trusted Jesus as their Savior continued to obey these special laws, which was all right. Unfortunately, they also continued to look down on Gentiles, believing that salvation through Jesus Christ was only for Jewish people—God's chosen people.

2. God's plan for the Gentiles.

(MAP OF ISRAEL)
Do you remember the command Jesus gave to his disciples before he went back to heaven? Yes, he told them to take the gospel to all the world. ▲#4 Had they obeyed him? Yes and no. They had gone from Jerusalem to Judea and then to Samaria *(display the map and indicate places as you mention them)*, but no further. They had told other Jews about Jesus, but not their Gentile neighbors. Since the people in the rest of the world were mostly Gentiles, the Jewish believers were not too excited about preaching the gospel in those places. ▲#5

But God wanted these Jewish believers to understand this important truth—that the Lord Jesus wanted them to take the good news about him to all the world. Because the early Church looked up to Peter as one of their leaders, God taught him this lesson first.

**3. Cornelius worships God.
(Acts 9:43-10:8)**

(MAP OF ISRAEL; Cornelius 68, angel 7A)
After Peter raised Dorcas from the dead, he stayed for a while in Joppa *(indicate on the map)* with a believer named Simon who lived near the sea.

A Roman soldier named Cornelius *(place 68 on the board)* lived in the town of Caesarea about 40 miles up the coast *(indicate on map)*. Cornelius was a centurion, which meant that he was a captain in charge of 100 soldiers in the Roman army. He was a Roman and a Gentile, but he did not worship idols like many of the other Romans did. Instead, the Bible tells us, he and his family worshiped the one true God and prayed to him every day. Cornelius was a kind and generous man who gave gifts to the poor, but apparently he had never heard about Jesus and salvation.

One afternoon while Cornelius was praying, an angel *(add 7A)* in shining clothing appeared before him and spoke his name: "Cornelius."

Cornelius was afraid and said, "What is it, sir?"

The angel answered, "God has heard your prayers and seen the gifts you give to the poor. Now send some men to Joppa to find a man named Peter. He is staying in the home of Simon who lives by the sea." Then the angel left him. *(Remove 7A; leave 68 on the board.)*

(Servants 6D, soldier 32A)

Cornelius immediately called two of his trusted servants and a soldier who was also a worshiper of the true God *(add 6D, 32A)*. He told them about the angel's message and then said, "Go to Joppa and find this man. I must hear what he has to say!"

4. Peter learns a lesson.
(Acts 10:9-23)

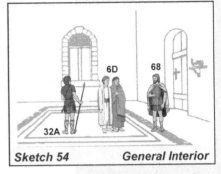

Sketch 54   General Interior

(Peter 69, sheet 70)

The next day about noon Peter *(place 69 on the board)* went up to the roof of Simon's home to pray. Many of the homes had flat roofs where the family could enjoy the cool breezes and look out over the beautiful blue sea. It was a good place for Peter to be alone with God. He had no idea that Cornelius' servants were on their way to find him.

As he was praying, Peter became hungry and wanted something to eat. While he was waiting for the meal to be prepared, God sent him a vision. Peter saw heaven opened and something like a large sheet *(add 70)* being let down to the earth by its four corners. In the sheet were all kinds of animals, reptiles and birds. Then a voice said to him, "Get up, Peter. Kill something and eat it."

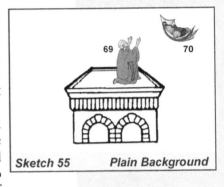

Sketch 55   Plain Background

But Peter said, "Oh, no, Lord! I have never eaten anything that is impure or unclean." Peter was reminding God that he had told the Jews many years before never to eat certain animals. In this sheet there were many of those "unclean" animals.

But the voice spoke to him again saying, "Do not call unclean anything that God has made clean." This happened three times and then the sheet was taken back to heaven.

(Servants 6D, soldier 32A, Peter 11)

As Peter was thinking about this strange sight and wondering what God was trying to teach him, the three men *(place 6D, 32A on the board)* from Cornelius arrived at the front gate and called out, "Is a man called Peter staying here?"

At the same time the Holy Spirit was saying to Peter, "Three men are looking for you. I want you to go with them. I have sent them to you."

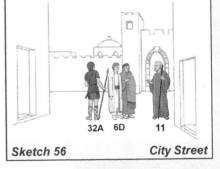

Sketch 56   City Street

So Peter *(add 11)* went downstairs and said to the men, "I am Peter. Why have you come?"

"We have come from Cornelius, the Roman centurion in Caesarea," they answered. "An angel told him to send for you and to listen to what you have to say."

Peter invited them in to spend the night, even though Jews would not normally have a Gentile in their homes. The next day he and some believers from Joppa traveled with them back to Cornelius' home in Caesarea.

5. Peter teaches Cornelius and other Gentiles. (Acts 10:24-48)

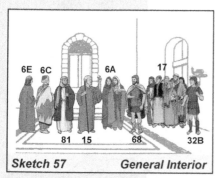

Sketch 57   General Interior

(Cornelius 68, women 6A, men 6C, 6E, 81, crowd 17, soldier 32B, Peter 15)

Place 68, 6A, 6C, 6E, 81, 17, 32B on the board.

When Peter *(add 15)* and the others arrived at Cornelius' home, a crowd of people was waiting. Cornelius had invited some of his relatives and friends to hear what Peter had to say. Cornelius knelt down at Peter's feet as if to worship him. Peter said, "Stand up! I am only a man like you."

Then Peter said, "You know that it is against our law for Jews to have anything to do with people who are not Jews. But God has shown me that I must not feel that way anymore, so I came as you asked. Why have you sent for me?"

Cornelius answered, "Four days ago when I was praying a man in bright clothing suddenly stood before me. He told me to send for you, so I did. I am glad you have come. We have gathered to hear what God has to say to us through you."

Peter said to them, "I know now that God does not show favoritism, but accepts all who come to him by faith in Christ Jesus. And I know now that Jesus died for you Gentiles just as he died for us." Then he told them about the Lord Jesus and his death and resurrection.

Before Peter had finished speaking, the Holy Spirit came upon Cornelius and his friends, just as he had upon the disciples on the day of Pentecost. They began to praise God in different languages, just as the disciples had done. Peter and the Jewish Christians who were with him were astonished when they saw this happening. It was God's way of showing them that he accepted the Gentiles as well as the Jews when they came to him by faith in Christ Jesus. So Peter learned that day that the Church is made up of both Jews and Gentiles, and that God wants believers to take the good news about Jesus to everyone in the world.

The new believers were baptized with water in the name of the Lord Jesus Christ to show that they believed in him. Peter stayed with them for several days to teach them more about the Savior.

Conclusion

Summary

(Peter 11, JEW 73, GENTILE 73, sheet 70)

What was Peter's problem? *(Place 11 on the board; encourage response throughout.)* He was like other early Jewish believers *(add JEW 73)* who still kept the Old Testament laws and would not have anything to do with the Gentile people around them *(add GENTILE 73)* who did not keep the laws. He did not believe that the good news about Jesus was for the Gentiles.

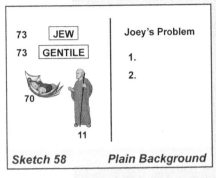

Sketch 58   Plain Background

What lesson did God teach Peter about this? Yes, that he was to share the good news about Jesus with all people, no matter how different or strange they seemed.

How did God teach Peter this lesson? That's right; God spoke to him three times in a vision *(add 70)*, saying, "Don't call anything impure that God has made clean."

How did Peter show that he had learned what God was teaching him? He went immediately to Cornelius' house and taught the Gentiles God's Word.

Application

(Newsprint & marker)

Do you remember Joey and his problem? *(Briefly review the introductory story; allow for response throughout.)* How did Joey's friends treat the new boys? Yes, they called them losers and tried to keep them off their team. What are some other ways we sometimes treat people who are different? *(You may suggest ignoring or avoiding them or joining in with others who make fun of them.)*

What do you think Joey should do? What does God want Joey to do? *(Discuss and print responses on newsprint you have attached to the right side of the board.)*

Will it be easy for Joey to obey God and show his love to the new boys? *(Response)* No, it won't. Then how can Joey do it? *(Response)* Yes, he must first pray and ask God to help him. Because he has trusted Jesus as his Savior the Holy Spirit lives in him to help him. Then he can spend some time getting to know the boys, perhaps talking with them on the playground or walking home with them. He can choose them to be on his team, no matter what the others say, and help them learn to play ball better. In this way he will be showing God's love to them and someday may be able to tell them that Jesus loves them and died for them, too. By accepting them and helping them he will also be demonstrating God's love to the other boys on his team.

What about you? Are you like Peter or Joey? Do you find it difficult to accept others who are different from you? Sometimes it seems easier to dislike, ignore or mistreat people who are from another country or speak another language or have different customs from our own—or people who misbehave because they feel left out or those who are physically or mentally challenged. We are often afraid of those who are different from us because we don't understand them. If you know Jesus as your Savior, God wants to help you accept people as those Jesus died for and show kindness to them, whether they are like you or different. By doing this you can show them that God loves them.

Today will you decide that from now on you will trust God to help you accept people as ones Jesus died for and treat them in a way that would show them God's love so that you may someday tell them the good news about Jesus?

Response Activity

*Distribute the **"A Plan for Accepting Others" handouts** and pencils. Read through the handout aloud with the children. Give them opportunity to ask questions or make comments to ascertain if they understand the commitment they would be making.* ▲#6

Give opportunity for the children to think and pray quietly, asking God for help to make and keep this commitment. Then ask those who choose to do so to sign the form. Have them all take the forms home as a reminder to put these things into practice this week. Encourage any who do not sign it today to pray about it and sign it when they are ready.

Close in prayer, asking God to help everyone there to accept people and speak to them about God's love.

Next week ask if any had opportunity to keep their promise and encourage them to share what happened.

✍ TAKE HOME ITEMS

*Distribute **memory verse tokens for Romans 3:22, 23** and **Bible Study Helps for Lesson 10**.*

▲ **Option #6**

Have children put a ✓ beside 1 or 2 things on the response form that they know they need to work on this week rather than trying to do the whole list to start with.

An Angel Frees Peter from Prison
Theme: Prayer

Lesson 11

❋ BEFORE YOU BEGIN...

What is prayer? Does God really hear us when we pray? And if he hears, does he answer? Why does he seem to answer some prayers, but not others? How does God answer prayer?

Have you ever asked such questions? Most of us have. Your children probably have as well. They need to understand what prayer is and how important it is. They need to learn how to pray. They also need to understand how God longs for them to come and talk with him—and that he will answer them, though not always as they desire.

Use this story of God's miracle-working for Peter in answer to the believers' prayers to encourage your class to believe that God *does* hear and answer prayer. Through the remainder of the lesson, teach them that God does not always answer *yes* and that his other answers are meant for our ultimate good. Use this lesson to help your boys and girls begin to pray regularly for specific people or requests. *"And all things, whatever you ask in prayer, believing, you will receive" (Matthew 21:22, NKJV).*

☞ AIM:

That the children may

- Know that God answers the prayers of those who have trusted Jesus as Savior.
- Respond by beginning a daily prayer time and praying for specific requests.

📖 SCRIPTURE: Acts 12:1-23

♥ MEMORY VERSE: 1 Peter 3:12

For the eyes of the Lord are over the righteous, and his ears are open unto their prayers: but the face of the Lord is against them that do evil. (KJV)

For the eyes of the Lord are on the righteous and his ears are attentive to their prayer, but the face of the Lord is against those who do evil. (NIV)

📁 MATERIALS TO GATHER

Memory verse visual for 1 Peter 3:12
Backgrounds: Review Chart, Plain Background, Council Room, Temple, Prison, City Street, General Interior
Figures: 1R(2), R1-R11, 6A, 6B, 6E, 7A, 7B, 14, 29 32A, 32B, 37, 38, 43, 44, 61, 74, 75, 76, 77A, 77B, 77C, 78
Token holders & memory verse tokens for 1 Peter 3:12
Bible Study Helps for Lesson 11
Special:
- *For Review Chart:* Memory verse visuals for 1 Peter 1:22, Romans 3:22, 23; newsprint & marker or chalkboard & chalk
- *For Introduction, Summary & Application:* Word cards YES, NO, WAIT
- *For Application:* Word strips PRAISE, CONFESS, REQUEST, THANK
- *For Response Activity:* "My Prayer Time" handouts, pencils
- *For Options:* Materials for any options you choose to use
- *Note:* To prepare word cards YES, NO, WAIT, print the following words in large letters on 9 x12-inch construction paper: YES on green, NO on red, and WAIT on yellow. Use as flashcards or back with flannel or felt to use on the felt board.

  Follow the instructions on page xii to make the word strips and the "My Prayer Time" handouts (pattern P-10 on page 143).

🏠 REVIEW CHART

Display the Review Chart with 1R and R1-R8 in place. Have R9-R11 ready to use when indicated. Have the children review the last two lessons by giving the themes and placing R9 and R10 on the Chart. To review the memory verses for Lessons 9 and 10, display the visual pieces in random order, one verse at a time or both together. Allow the children to take turns putting them in proper order, one or two pieces at a time. Have the class recite each verse after it is unscrambled.

Use the following questions to review Lesson 10:

1. What is the name for God's special nation of people? *(Israel or the Jewish people)*
2. What did the Jewish people call those who were not from their nation? *(Gentiles)*
3. Who was Cornelius? *(A Roman centurion)*
4. How was Cornelius different from other Romans/Gentiles? *(He worshiped the true God.)*
5. What message did God give to Peter in the vision of the sheet and animals? *(That he was not to call unclean what God had called clean)*

6. Why did God give the vision of the sheet and the animals to Peter? *(So he would not think of the Gentiles as unclean and would take the gospel to them)*
7. How did God prepare Cornelius for Peter's coming? *(God sent an angel to him.)*
8. Explain in your own words what Romans 3:22, 23 means. *(Whatever people's differences might be, they all are sinners and must come to him to be saved from sin through faith in Jesus Christ.)*

Today's building block for our Life House is *Prayer (place R11 on Chart)*. Who can tell us what prayer is? *(Print responses on newsprint or chalkboard.)* Prayer is simply talking to God. How do we know he hears us? *(Response.)* Many people wonder about this. We will learn the answer to this question in our memory verse.

♥ MEMORY VERSE

Display the visual for 1 Peter 3:12.

Peter wrote these words to people who were being persecuted because they believed in Jesus as the Son of God. He wanted them to be encouraged by knowing that God had not forgotten them in their trouble. These same words can help us and teach us something about prayer.

This verse tells us three things about God. Let's see if we can discover what they are as we read it together. *(Read the verse in unison.)* Did you notice that it talks about God's eyes and ears and face? You know that God is a spirit and that he doesn't have a body like we have. Nevertheless, the Bible tells us that God is a real person because he thinks and feels and makes choices. Even without a body like ours, he can still see us and hear us. ▲#1

What is the first thing our verse tells us about God? *(Allow for response throughout.)* Yes, that his eyes "are over the righteous." He sees and watches over everyone who belongs to his family through accepting Jesus as Savior.

What is the next thing it tells us about God? Yes, "His ears are open unto their prayers"—he hears them when they pray. Whose prayers does God hear? The prayers of the righteous—those who have trusted in Jesus as Savior. ▲#2

What is the last thing our verse tells us about God? Correct, he turns his face away from those who do evil or sin. Can you tell from your mom's or dad's facial expression how they feel about something you have done wrong? These words don't mean that God doesn't know when people do wrong. Rather, they tell us how God feels about evil. He *turns away* from it because he is *against* it. He is holy and hates sin. But when sinners come to him for forgiveness through his Son, Jesus, then God's eyes will watch over them and his ears will hear their prayers.

▲ **Option #1**

Make word cards or strips for THINK, FEEL, CHOOSE.

▲ **Option #2**

Distribute paper and markers or crayons. Have the children illustrate their ideas of prayer. Then have them show their drawings to the class and explain their meaning.

▲ Option #3

Memorizing the verse: Use actions with the verse.

"For the eyes"
  point to eyes;

"of the Lord"
  point heavenward;

"are over (on) the righteous"
  place hand as visor over eyes and look down;

"and his ears"
  point to ears;

"are open (attentive)"
  cup ears;

"unto (to) their prayers:"
  hands in praying position;

"but the face"
  point face in one direction;

"of the Lord"
  point heavenward;

"is against them that (those who) do evil."
  put hands in a push-away position.

Prayer is simply talking to God in a natural way, but remembering that we are not talking to an equal, but to Almighty God. We can tell God anything: how wonderful he is, how much we love him, how thankful we are to him for all he does for us. Or, how happy or sad we are, how hard it is in school or the problems we have with friends or family. We can also confess our sin to him and accept his forgiveness. This is all possible because we belong to God's family through Jesus. *(Work on memorizing the verse.)* ▲#3

📖 BIBLE LESSON OUTLINE

An Angel Frees Peter from Prison

■ Introduction
  How God answers prayer

■ Bible Content
  1. Herod arrests Peter.
  2. The believers pray and God answers.
  3. The believers are surprised.
  4. God punishes Herod.

■ Conclusion
  Summary

  Application
    Learning how to pray

  Response Activity
    Praying for specific requests

📖 BIBLE LESSON

■ Introduction
  How God answers prayer

(Word cards YES, NO, WAIT)
Our memory verse tells us that God hears our prayers. Have you ever prayed to God? *(Allow for response throughout.)* Has God answered a prayer for you? What was the answer? Does God always give us what we ask for? If he doesn't, does it mean he has not answered?

We will use the colors of a traffic light to help us remember three different ways God answers prayer. *(Let children hold up word cards as they are mentioned.)* The green light means go. It reminds us that God sometimes says YES, giving us what we are asking for because he knows it is the best thing for us and the right time to have it. The red light means stop. It reminds us that sometimes God says NO. He answers no when he knows that what we are asking for would not be good for us. The yellow light means caution. It reminds us that sometimes God's answer is WAIT because it is not the best time to have what we are asking for. All three of these answers—yes, no, and wait—are answers to our prayer from God.

Let's listen to our story today to find out which of these three ways God answered the prayer of some believers.

■ Bible Content

1. **Herod arrests Peter.**
   (Acts 12:1-5a)

(Herod 74, soldiers 32A, 32B, 76, Jewish leaders 30, 31)
Place 74, 32A, 32B, 76 on the board.

During the days when the early Church was beginning to grow, Israel was ruled by King Herod Agrippa. He was the grandson of the wicked King Herod who was ruling when Jesus was born.

This King Herod was also very wicked and he decided to persecute the believers. He gave orders to arrest some of them, including their leaders. When he discovered that he had captured the apostle James, he gave orders for him to be killed.

Sketch 59 **Council Room/Temple**

The Jewish leaders *(add 30, 31)* were so pleased about James' death that Herod sent soldiers to arrest Peter and have him killed also. But because the Jews were celebrating Passover, Herod had Peter locked in prison, planning to have him killed when the celebration had ended.

2. **The believers pray and God answers.**
   (Acts 12:5b-11)

(Peter 77B, soldiers 77A, 77C, angel 7B)
Place 77B, 77A, 77C on the board.

It was nothing new for Peter to be in prison. He had been there at least twice before. One of those times an angel had released him. No doubt the people remembered this. Perhaps Herod did too. He wasn't going to chance Peter's escaping again, so he ordered sixteen soldiers, four at a time, to guard him. Two of the soldiers guarded the doors. The other two were chained to Peter. There was no way Peter could escape. Peter trusted God and waited to see what would happen. ▲#4

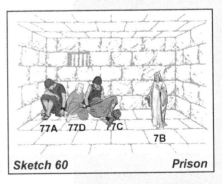

Sketch 60 **Prison**

▲ Option #4

Use drama as a method to tell this exciting story. Choose children to take the parts of Peter, the angel, the guards and the believers.

Create two scenes—a prison and the home of Mark—one on either side of the room.

Read Acts 12:5-17 aloud as the children act out the scenes.

Or, read the story aloud and then have the children create their own dialogue as they portray it.

The believers in Jerusalem knew what Herod was planning to do and that there was nothing they could do to change his mind. They also knew that God was able to rescue Peter, so they prayed for him continually. As they prayed, God answered their prayers in a very wonderful way.

Late at night after Passover had ended, Peter was sleeping peacefully in his jail cell even though Herod was planning to execute him the very next day. He knew that he would go at once to be with Jesus if he were killed, so he was not afraid. He was chained to two soldiers; they must have been sleeping too. Other guards were stationed at the door of the prison.

Suddenly an angel *(add 7B)* appeared and a light shone in the dark prison. The angel touched Peter on the side and said, "Get up quickly." Peter stood up and the chains fell off his wrists. He was free! How do you think he felt? *(Response)* The angel said, "Put on your coat and your sandals and follow me."

3. The believers are surprised. (Acts 12:12-17a)

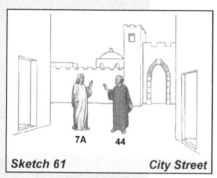

Sketch 61   **City Street**

(Peter 44, angel 7A)

Peter *(place 44 on the board)* followed the angel *(add 7A)*, but he wasn't sure if what was happening was real. They passed the first and second guard. Then they came to the big iron gate that led to the street and it opened by itself. They walked through the gate and down the street. Suddenly the angel was gone *(remove 7A)*.

Then Peter realized that this was no dream. He really was free! He thought, "Now I know that the Lord sent his angel to rescue me from Herod and from everything the Jews were hoping would happen."

Peter kept walking until he came to the home of one of the believers named Mary. She was the mother of John Mark who later became a missionary and wrote the Gospel According to Mark. There was a light in the house but the doors were tightly locked. Even though it was the middle of the night, many believers were on their knees praying for his release. Peter knocked on the door. *(Move 44 to door on left of scene.)*

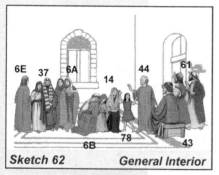

Sketch 62   **General Interior**

(Believers 6A, 6B, 6E, 14, 37, 43, 61, Rhoda 78, Peter 44)
Place 6A, 6B, 6E, 14, 37, 43, 61 on the board.

The people inside must have wondered who would be knocking at this time of night. Could it be soldiers coming to arrest more believers? Rhoda, a young servant girl, went to the door and called out, "Who is there?"

"It's Peter. Let me in." Rhoda was so excited and happy that she forgot to open the door! Instead, she left him standing outside while she *(add 78)* ran back into the house crying, "Peter is at the door."

"Why, it can't be!" some of the people said. "Peter is in prison. You must be crazy!"

"But it *is* Peter," Rhoda cried excitedly. "I know his voice. I'm sure it's Peter!"

Then someone said, "It must be his spirit. Perhaps Herod has put him to death already."

All this time Peter was standing outside knocking. Finally someone opened the door and let him in *(add 44)*. How surprised they all were to see him! They had prayed for him for many days, but they were surprised when God answered with a yes!

Quickly Peter asked them to be quiet. Then he described for them all that had happened and how the angel had delivered him. "Go tell James and the rest of the leaders about the wonderful thing that God has done!" (This James was a half-brother of the Lord Jesus and now a leader in the church at Jerusalem.) Then Peter left them and went to another place. He knew that Herod would search for him as soon as he found out that he was missing from the prison.

4. God punishes Herod.
   (Acts 12:17b-23)

(Herod 74, soldier 32B, soldiers 76, 32A, crowd 29, man 38, men 75)

The next morning there was a lot of excitement at the prison! The soldiers who had been chained to Peter still had the chains on their wrists, but Peter was gone! The guards were still outside the door, but they hadn't seen or heard Peter all night! No one had any idea what had happened.

King Herod was furious *(place 74, 32B on the board)*. He searched everywhere, but could not find Peter. He questioned all the guards *(add 76, 32A)*, but could get no answers. Peter had simply disappeared. In his fury Herod commanded that all the guards be put to death for letting Peter escape *(remove 76, 32A)*. Herod really was a wicked man!

Sketch 63   Council Room/Temple

Soon after this, the king went to Caesarea, a city on the coast. He put on his royal robes, sat on his throne and made a speech to people *(add 29, 38, 75)* from nearby cities. They all shouted, "This is the voice of a god and not a man!" They knew better, but they were trying to make the king feel important. Because Herod accepted the people's worship and praise and refused to give the honor to God, an angel of God caused him to become very ill. He soon died from a dreadful disease.

But God's Word did not die. The good news about Jesus spread rapidly and the Church continued to grow. Many people believed in Jesus because they had seen God's power in action.

Conclusion

Summary

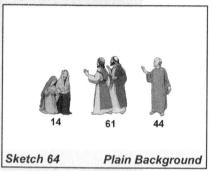

Sketch 64 — Plain Background

(Word cards YES, NO, WAIT; believers 61, 14, Peter 44)
Review the YES, NO and WAIT answers to prayer by having volunteers hold the cards as they explain each one.

What answer to prayer did God give to the believers we heard about today? *(Place 61, 14 on the board; encourage response throughout. Have a child choose the correct card from the table and hold it up.)* That is correct; he answered "yes" when he freed Peter from prison *(add 44)*.

How did God free Peter? Yes, he sent an angel who led Peter out of the prison without the guards hearing a thing. It was a miracle!

Why would God answer in such an incredible way? That's right; he wanted his people to know that he was watching over them and hearing them when they prayed. This was especially encouraging to them at this time when some of them were being persecuted for their faith in Jesus Christ. God doesn't always do miraculous things when we pray, but he always hears and cares. He still has the power to do exciting and wonderful things. *(Remove all the figures.)*

Application

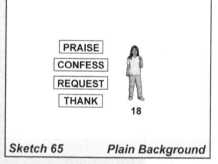

Sketch 65 — Plain Background

(Girl 18; word cards YES, NO, WAIT; word strips PRAISE, CONFESS, REQUEST, THANK)
Our memory verse reminds us that God answers prayer. Let's say it together once more. *(Do so.)* If you *(place 18 on the board)* are one of the "righteous"—those who belong to God's family because they have accepted Jesus as Savior—then God has promised to hear and answer your prayers. Has God ever answered one of your prayers with a yes? *(Display the YES card; encourage response throughout.)*

Maybe you have been praying about something and think God has not heard you because you haven't had an answer. It may be that he is saying WAIT *(display the WAIT card)* because it's not the right time yet. Or he might be saying NO *(display the NO card)* because he knows it is best *not* to give you what you're asking for.

Perhaps you've never taken time to pray because you don't belong to God's family. But you can change that today. God always hears the prayers of those who come to him confessing their sin and asking Jesus to be their Savior. When you receive Jesus as your Savior, you are become part of the family of God. Then you can begin praying—or talking with God—every day.

Or perhaps you are in God's family, but you don't pray very much. God loves to hear his children pray. Talk to him just as though he is your best friend. Talk to him anytime—morning, noon or night. And talk to him anyplace—at school, on the playground, at home, walking to school, even in your bed. He hears you when you pray silently or out loud.

Praise *(add PRAISE)* God for who he is; tell him he is wonderful and that you love him.

As God's child confess *(add CONFESS)* to God when you sin and accept his forgiveness through Jesus.

Request *(add REQUEST)* or ask things from God, praying for our nation, for the leaders of our country, for your parents and teachers and friends. Ask God to help you obey him every day, to help you with your homework, to provide a job for your father or help someone who is ill. And ask God to help you be faithful to pray to him every day.

Thank *(add THANK)* God for his answers to your prayers, for taking care of you, for providing your needs, for everything he does for all of us! God is very pleased when we thank him! Let's take a minute just to thank God right now for who he is and all he does for us. *(Do so.)*

Response Activity

*Encourage the children to begin having a prayer time each day and to pray for specific requests. Distribute the **"My Prayer Time" handouts** and pencils and have the children sign their name. Explain how they should use the handout: to first praise God; then confess any sin to God; then print specific requests on the paper with the date they began to pray and then pray for them each day. Show them where they can print the date God answers their prayer and the kind of answer it was.*

Emphasize the importance of giving thanks to God for hearing their prayer as well as for answering it.

Remind the children that the first prayer we need to pray is to receive Jesus as our Savior. Invite any who have not yet done this to pray silently right now, admitting they are sinners and asking Jesus to forgive them and be their Savior. Then pray for them in your closing prayer and ask them to come and talk with you after class.

✍ TAKE HOME ITEMS

*Distribute **memory verse tokens for 1 Peter 3:12** and **Bible Study Helps for Lesson 11**.*

The First Missionaries Are Sent
Theme: Witnessing

Lesson 12

Part One: Barnabas & Saul Go to Cyprus

❋ BEFORE YOU BEGIN...

What will I do when I grow up? How can I know what I should be? What's going to happen to our world? Probably some of your children are already asking these questions, especially the older ones. In a world that offers little hope politically, economically or in the general state of affairs, it is easy to succumb to hopelessness, to feel there is no meaningful place for them. For this reason it is increasingly important for boys and girls to know that God has a plan for each one of his children as well as a plan for our world to hear the gospel message. He knows what each child is to become and desires that they all will witness for him throughout their lives in order to spread the good news about Jesus.

Use this lesson to teach these basic truths. Challenge them to be willing witnesses right in their own "world" by living and speaking up for Jesus Christ. Help them see the importance of being a witness for Jesus wherever they are so that others can believe the wonderful good news of Jesus' death and resurrection to provide salvation for them, too. *"For we are His workmanship, created in Christ Jesus for good works, which God prepared beforehand that we should walk in them" (Ephesians 2:10, NKJV).*

☞ AIM:

That the children may

- Know that God wants every Christian to be a witness for Jesus Christ.
- Respond by choosing someone they will pray for and plan to witness to about Jesus this week.

📖 SCRIPTURE: Acts 11:19-30; 12:25–13:12

♥ MEMORY VERSE: John 3:17

For God sent not his Son into the world to condemn the world, but that the world through him might be saved. (KJV)

For God did not send his Son into the world to condemn the world, but to save the world through him. (NIV)

MATERIALS TO GATHER

Memory verse visual for John 3:17
Backgrounds: Review Chart, Plain Background, Plain Interior, General Interior, Council Room/Temple
Figures: 1R, R1-R12, 5, 6A, 6C, 6D, 6E, 12, 13, 18, 43, 71, 80, 81, 82, 83, 84
Token holders & memory verse tokens for John 3:17
Bible Study Helps for Lesson 12, Part One
Special:
- *For Review Chart:* Word strip WITNESS
- *For Introduction:* Word strip WITNESS; newsprint & marker or chalkboard & chalk
- *For Bible Content 1:* MAP OF ISRAEL from Lesson 7
- *For Bible Content 2:* Word strip CHRISTIAN
- *For Bible Content 4:* "PAUL'S JOURNEYS MAP" poster ⌂**(1)**
- *For Summary:* Word strip WITNESS
- *For Application:* Word strip CHRISTIAN; newsprint & marker or chalkboard & chalk
- *For Response Activity:* Paper or 4 x 6-inch cards, pencils; word strip WITNESS
- *For Options:* Materials for any options you choose to use
- *Note: Follow the instructions on page xii to prepare the word strips.*

  To prepare the "Paul's Journeys Map" poster, enlarge the map (pattern P-2 on page 139) on heavy-weight poster board for use throughout the remaining lessons in this volume.

⌂ **Note (1)**

PAUL'S JOURNEYS MAP background may be purchased from BCM Publications.

 REVIEW CHART

Display the Review Chart with 1R and R1-R11 in place. Briefly review the theme and memory verse from Lesson 11, having the child who says the verse place the symbol on the Chart. Have R12 and word strip WITNESS ready for use as indicated.

To review the last few lessons, ask for volunteers who will pretend to be one of the characters you have already studied. Use the questions below (and/or questions you or the children write) to interview the volunteer characters. ▲#1

▲ **Option #1**

Provide a costume for each child who plays a character.

CORNELIUS:
1. Why did you send for Peter to come to your home? *(God's angel told me to send for him.)*
2. What happened in your family after Peter met with you? *(We believed in Jesus as Savior and were baptized.)*

⌂ **Note (2)**

Perhaps comparing our witnessing for Jesus to being a character witness in court—something they may frequently see on TV—would help your children understand this concept.

▲ **Option #2**

Before displaying the verse visual, have the children find the verse in their Bibles. Ask different children to read the parts of the verse as you come to them, and others to answer your questions. Then display the verse visual and read the whole verse aloud as a group.

DORCAS:
1. Tell us why so many people loved you and spoke well of you. *(I made clothes for the poor in my town and helped those in need.)*
2. What miracle did God do for you? *(He raised me from the dead.)*

RHODA:
1. Why were you and the other believers meeting in John Mark's home? *(We were praying for Peter to be released from prison.)*
2. What surprise did you receive when you went to answer a knock on the door? *(Peter was out of prison and standing at the door.)*

PETER:
1. What difficult lesson did God teach you about the Gentiles? *(That I needed to accept them and tell them about Jesus)*
2. How did God teach you this lesson? *(He spoke to me through a vision of a sheet filled with many kinds of animals and then sent me to Cornelius' home.)*

Our new building block is called *Witnessing (place R12 on the Chart).* We can see the word witness in this word *(add word strip WITNESS and compare it with the building block).* Witnessing about Jesus is one of the things God wants us to "build" into our lives. We will learn more about this word in our lesson today. ⌂**(2)**

♥ **MEMORY VERSE**

Use the verse visual to teach John 3:17.

Our verse tells us two important things about Jesus *(display the verse visual.)* What is the first one? *(Allow for response throughout.)* That's right! Jesus did not come to condemn the world. ▲**#2**

We often hear that a judge has condemned a person or sentenced him to a punishment for a crime. We have learned that every person is a sinner and deserves to be punished. God says that the punishment for sin is to be separated from him forever in a place called hell. But God did not send Jesus to sentence us to that punishment. Let's say the first part of our verse together.

Now look at the second important truth our verse tells us about Jesus. Why did he come? Yes, he came to *save* the world! Who can tell us how Jesus did this? *(Response)* He died on the cross to take the punishment for our sin and rose from the dead to be our living Savior. He could do this because he was the perfect and sinless Son of God. Let's say the second part of our verse together.

What must we do so we will not be condemned for our sin? *(Allow children to express what they know of the plan of salvation.)* We must 1) admit that we are sinners, 2) believe Jesus died and rose again from the dead for us, and 3) choose to receive Jesus as our Savior.

When we do this, what does God do for us? He forgives us and takes away our guilt as sinners. We become his child and receive the gift of eternal life. At that moment the Holy Spirit comes to live in us to help us live a life that pleases God.

This is the wonderful good news God wants us to share as we "witness" to our friends or to people anywhere we go! *(Work on memorizing the verse.)* ▲#3

📖 BIBLE LESSON OUTLINE

Barnabas & Saul Go to Cyprus

■ Introduction
What is a witness?

■ Bible Content
1. Believers witness faithfully in Antioch.
2. Barnabas comes to help the believers.
3. The church sends Barnabas and Saul to Cyprus.
4. God blesses witnessing on Cyprus.

■ Conclusion
Summary

Application
   Being a witness

Response Activity
   Choosing someone to witness to and a way to do it

📖 BIBLE LESSON

■ Introduction
What is a witness?

(Review Chart with R12 in place, word strip WITNESS, newsprint & marker or chalkboard & chalk)

Who can tell us what this word witness *(place WITNESS on the Review Chart)* means? *(Response)* That's correct. A witness is someone who sees or hears something and/or tells what they know about what they saw or heard. ▲#4

Have you ever had to do that? What did you witness and then who did you tell about it? *(Allow children to share experiences. Stimulate thinking with examples—a fight on the playground, an accident or a sports event.)* As a witness to the event you had to tell exactly all you saw and heard so that others would know what happened. You were witnessing about the event to others who had not been there.

▲ Option #3

Memorizing the verse: Distribute the visual pieces to seven children. Have them display their pieces—one at a time—in the proper order, with the class repeating the words aloud each time a piece is added.

When the verse is complete, have them repeat the entire verse.

Distribute the verse pieces to another set of children and have them, on a given signal, run to the front and line themselves in order across the room.

Continue with a different group until all have an opportunity to participate. Time each group to see which can do it the quickest.

Have the class repeat the verse each time it is displayed.

▲ Option #4

Definition Word Card: Witness = To see or hear something; to tell what you know about what you saw or heard.

🏠 **Note (3)**

The term *Christian* was first used in derision by the unbelieving crowd in Antioch. However, its negative beginning gave way to a more respectful identification of those who seriously follow the Lord Jesus.

In these days, unfortunately, the term is used to include such a wide spectrum of people that it clouds the biblical concept. We find ourselves having to say "a *real* Christian." Carefully guide your children to discern that in God's sight only a true believer in Jesus Christ is a Christian so they will not mistakenly judge that everyone who claims to be one is truly a committed follower of Christ.

God wants us to build witnessing into our Life House *(indicate WITNESS)*. What or who are we to be witnessing about? Yes, God's Son, the Lord Jesus. But how are we to do that since we have never actually seen Jesus or heard him teach? *(Response)* We know about him through what we read in the Bible and because we have received him as our Savior. God the Holy Spirit who lives in us will help us witness—or talk—to others about who Jesus is, what we know to be true about him and what he has done for us personally. In this way people who do not know Jesus can hear about him and have a chance to believe in him as their Savior.

What are some of the things we can tell about Jesus? *(Encourage response. If necessary, suggest basic facts like, Jesus was born and lived on the earth, he loves all of us and wants us to belong to God's family, he died so we can have our sin forgiven, he rose again from the dead, specific examples of how he has helped them. List responses on newsprint or chalkboard. These responses should give you insight into what your children actually know about Jesus and how correct their information is.)*

Where can we be a witness for Jesus? *(Response)* We can tell about Jesus at home or at school or in our neighborhood. Anywhere we go we can be witnesses by our words and by the way we live.

Today we will learn about two men who were witnesses for Jesus. Let's discover where they went and what happened.

■ **Bible Content**

1. Believers faithfully witness in Antioch. (Acts 11:19-21)

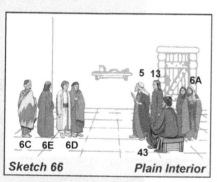

Sketch 66   Plain Interior

(Believers 5, 6C, 13, 6A, 6D, 6E, 43; MAP OF ISRAEL)
Sometimes God allows difficult things to happen to help us do what is right. Before Jesus returned to heaven, he said that he wanted his people to take the gospel to other places, but no one had gone. After Stephen was stoned, Saul and others began to persecute the believers in Jerusalem. As a result, many of them traveled long distances to find safer places to live, and wherever they went they witnessed about Jesus. They realized that God wants all believers to tell others the good news about Jesus' death and resurrection.

Some of the believers *(place 5, 6C, 13, 6A on the board)* from Jerusalem settled in Antioch *(indicate on the map)*, a large city in the country we now call Syria, on the seacoast far north of Jerusalem. At first they witnessed only to their Jewish neighbors and friends, but after a while, some of them began to tell the Gentiles about Jesus, too. In a very short time many people *(add 6D, 6E, 43)* heard about the Lord Jesus and believed in him as their Savior. God uses ordinary people who believe in Jesus and faithfully witness for him. *(Leave all the figures on the board.)*

2. Barnabas comes to help the believers.
   (Acts 11:22-26)

(Barnabas 80, Saul 84; word strip CHRISTIAN)
When the apostles and church leaders in Jerusalem heard what was happening in Antioch, they sent a man named Barnabas *(add 80)* to check on things and to help the new church. Barnabas was a good man who trusted and obeyed God. He had been one of the church leaders in Jerusalem from its very beginning. You will remember that he sold some land and brought the money to the apostles to help believers who were in need.

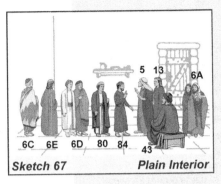

Sketch 67 — Plain Interior

Barnabas was glad to see the great work God was doing, bringing many people—both Jews and Gentiles—to believe in Jesus. He stayed there to teach the believers and encourage them to remain true to the Lord. Day by day, more and more people believed in the Lord.

Barnabas soon realized he needed someone to help him teach and organize all these people. Who would that be? He remembered Saul who had gone back to his home town of Tarsus, which was not far away. ▲#5

▲ **Option #5**

Show the location of Tarsus on the map. Note that it was in the area of modern-day Turkey.

Barnabas had been a friend to Saul when Saul first believed in Jesus as the Son of God. He knew that Saul had real ability to teach the Word of God and would be the perfect one to help with the Antioch church, so he went to Tarsus to look for him *(remove 80)*.

When Saul heard about the need, he gladly went back to Antioch with Barnabas *(add 80, 84)*. For a whole year both of these men taught and encouraged the new believers in the church, and the church continued to grow.

We read here in the book of Acts that Antioch is the place where believers were first called by the name *Christian (display word strip)*, which means "follower of Christ." From that time until now, that name has been given to those who trust Jesus Christ as Savior. ◿(3)

3. The church sends Barnabas and Saul to Cyprus.
   (Acts 13:1-3)

(Believers 5, 6C, 81, 13, Barnabas 80, Saul 84)
As time passed other men besides Barnabas and Saul also became leaders in the church in Antioch. One day as these leaders were all worshiping the Lord together *(place 5, 6C, 81, 13, 80, 84 on the board)*, God communicated with them. We don't know exactly how, but the Bible says that he said, "Set apart Barnabas and Saul *(indicate 80, 84)* to do the work I have called them to do." God wanted them to be his special witnesses to go to other places to spread the good news about Jesus.

Sketch 68 — General Interior

It must have been hard for the church people to see Barnabas and Saul go. They probably had learned to love them and appreciate their teaching and encouragement. But they wanted to obey God, so the leaders gathered round their dear friends and prayed that God would protect them in their travels and help them in their preaching.

4. God blesses witnessing on Cyprus. (Acts 13:4-12)

("PAUL'S JOURNEYS MAP" poster) ▲#6

Saul and Barnabas said their good-byes, boarded a ship, and sailed for the large island of Cyprus *(indicate on the map)* in the Mediterranean Sea. It was the country where Barnabas had been born and raised (Acts 4:36). Barnabas' nephew, John Mark, went with them as their helper. On Cyprus they preached the word of God in the Jewish synagogues. ◹**(4)** And day after day they walked around the island, preaching and teaching God's Word. They were witnessing about Jesus, saying that people needed to believe that he died on the cross for their sins and rose from the dead to save them.

(Governor 82, Elymas 83, Barnabas 80, John Mark 81, Saul 84)

Place 82, 83 on the board.

At Paphos, the very last place they visited, the Roman governor asked them to come and meet with him *(add 80, 81, 84)*. Look in verse seven to find why he sent for them. *(Response)* Yes, the Bible says he was an intelligent man and wanted to hear the Word of God. Saul and Barnabas immediately went to his house. There they discovered that a man named Elymas was with the governor.

Elymas was a sorcerer—something like a witch or a fortune teller. Look in verse eight to find what Elymas tried to do. *(Response)* Yes, he angrily interrupted Barnabas and Saul and tried to convince the governor not to listen to them. Why would Elymas do such a rude thing? That's right; he did not want the governor to believe God's Word.

Elymas did not believe in God or get his power from God. He served God's enemy, Satan. And Satan gave him the power to do special things to impress the people. Satan knows that if people believe in Jesus as Savior, he will no longer have power over them, so he works very hard to keep them from hearing the good news. Satan tried to use Elymas to keep Barnabas and Saul from telling the governor about Jesus. Satan will try to use other people to keep you from witnessing, too.

But the Holy Spirit living in Saul—who from this point on is called Paul—told him that Satan was using Elymas. Let's read Acts 13:9-11 to see what Paul did. *(Ask three different children to read these three verses aloud.)* Paul looked straight at Elymas and said, "You are a child

---

◹ **Note (4)**

A *synagogue* is a place where Jews and Gentile converts meet on the Sabbath (Saturday) to worship God and study the Old Testament. There was often a school in the synagogue where young boys came during the week to learn how to read and understand Scriptures.

Synagogues began after the Jewish people returned from captivity and were a significant part of Jewish worship in New Testament times.

Synagogues differed from the temple in two essential ways: there was only one temple, but there were many synagogues; and animal sacrifices could be offered only at the temple, never in a synagogue. A synagogue could be started whenever there were 12 adult males to meet together.

Sketch 69   Council Room/Temple

of Satan, the enemy of all that is good and right. You are full of evil and lies. Now the Lord is going to touch you and you will be blind for a while—not even able to see the sunlight."

Immediately Elymas lost his sight and groped around, trying to find someone to lead him by the hand. When the governor saw that happen, he believed. He was amazed by what he saw and by the teaching he had heard about the Lord Jesus Christ.

Paul and Barnabas must have been thrilled and excited by what God had done as they faithfully witnessed on Cyprus. They probably prayed, as they left the governor's house, that he would be a strong witness for the Lord Jesus there on the island after they were gone.

■ Conclusion

Summary

(Paul 84, Barnabas 80, governor 82, word strip WITNESS)

Where did God send Paul and Barnabas? *(Place 84, 80 on the board; encourage response throughout.)* Yes, to the island of Cyprus. What did they do on the island? They witnessed for Jesus *(add WITNESS)*.

Who remembers what a witness is? Yes, it's someone who tells what he knows about someone or something. When they witnessed, what did they tell people about Jesus? Yes, they told everybody about Jesus' death and resurrection and that they must believe in him to be saved and have their sins forgiven.

Who asked them to come and witness to him? Yes, the governor *(add 82)* of the island. What happened as a result? The governor became a Christian and Satan's power was defeated. How do you suppose Paul and Barnabas felt when they saw what God did? Do you think it made them want to continue witnessing about Jesus?

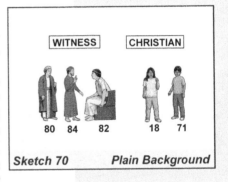

Sketch 70   Plain Background

Application

(Boy 71, girl 18; word strip CHRISTIAN; newsprint & marker or chalkboard & chalk)

If you *(add 71, 18)* are a Christian *(add CHRISTIAN)*, God wants you to be a witness for him to your friends who do not know Jesus. Can you think of someone you know who is not a believer in Jesus? Maybe someone in your family or at school or in your neighborhood? Are you willing to pray and ask God to help you witness to that person?

What are some ways we can be a witness? *(Encourage response. If necessary, suggest the following: invite others to Bible club or Sunday school, be Christ-like in the way we speak and act, tell how Jesus helps us, give a tract. List the children's responses on newsprint or chalkboard.)*
▲#7

▲ Option #6

For older children: Use a copy machine to duplicate the Paul's Journeys Map (pattern P-2, page 139). Hand them out along with crayons or colored markers so children can mark the route of Paul's travels in this and coming lessons.

Have the children print their name on their map and hand them in at the end of class so they will be able to use them for the next lesson.

▲ Option #7

Put the children in pairs or small groups. Give them a set period of time to prepare a skit demonstrating a way they could witness to someone. Then have each group present their skit to the class.

▲ Option #8

For younger children: Hand out paper and crayons or markers. Have the children draw a picture of a cross and a tomb with the stone rolled away. Then encourage them to take the picture to someone and tell them what it means.

▲ Option #9

Before class, print these two instructions on newsprint or chalkboard.
"Print on your card:
1. the name of the person you're thinking of;
2. how you will witness to that person this week."

In class, display so the children can remember them and do it.

Response Activity ▲#8

Lead the children to think specifically of someone to whom they can witness this week and pray silently for that person to believe in Jesus as Savior.

Distribute paper or 4 x 6-inch cards and pencils. Have them print 1) the name of the person they're thinking of and 2) how they will witness about Jesus to that person this week. Have them choose an idea from the list of suggestions made during the Application time or something else they have thought of.   ▲#9

Tell them to keep the card in their Bible or put it where they will see it at home and use it as a reminder to pray for and witness to the person.

Have children's tracts and invitations to your class available for those children who wish to use them.

Remind the children that they cannot be a witness for Jesus if they have not received him as their own Savior. Invite any who are not sure they are Christians to put their trust in him today and come speak with you about it after class.

Close in prayer asking God to help them carry out their plan to witness this week.

✍ TAKE HOME ITEMS

Distribute **memory verse tokens for John 3:17** and **Bible Study Helps for Lesson 12, Part One.**

The First Missionaries Are Sent
Theme: Witnessing

Part Two: Paul & Barnabas Go to Galatia

Lesson 12

 **BEFORE YOU BEGIN...**

Today our children are learning—by word and by example—that their most important goal in life should be to grow up, get a good job and make lots of money so they can be successful and live well. Unfortunately, this philosophy spills over into the Christian world. Because having financial security and a well-padded bank account are such important goals, it is difficult for Christians to think of entering missionary service and totally trusting God to meet their needs. Consequently, the world-wide missionary force is shrinking dramatically while the world's population is exploding. Still the Lord says, "Go ye into all the world and preach the gospel!"

Paul and Barnabas are outstanding examples of how God protects, strengthens and uses those who are willing to obey his command, and how he provides his servants' needs, physically and spiritually. Through this lesson challenge your children to begin witnessing now and also to consider giving their lives to serve God in the future as career missionaries. Show them how they can begin preparing while they are young for whatever God has planned for them in the future. And encourage them to be open to God's call, willing to say yes to his will for their lives. *"For I know the thoughts that I think toward you, says the LORD, thoughts of peace and not of evil, to give you a future and a hope" (Jeremiah 29:11, NKJV).*

👉 AIM:

That the children may

- Know that it is God's plan for some Christians to serve God as missionaries.
- Respond by offering themselves to God to serve him now and to prepare to serve him in the future.

📖 SCRIPTURE: Acts 13:13-52; Galatians 4:12-16

♥ MEMORY VERSE: John 3:17

For God sent not his Son into the world to condemn the world; but that the world through him might be saved. (KJV)

For God did not send his Son into the world to condemn the world, but to save the world through him. (NIV)

▲ Option #1

Reviewing the verse: Use the following games to review the verse.

1. Scramble the visual pieces on the felt board. Have the children take turns placing the pieces in correct order while the rest of the class checks to be sure they are correct.

2. Print each word of the verse on separate paper plates. Scatter the plates, facedown around the classroom. Divide the class into two groups and have them take turns finding the plates and putting them in order across the floor. Time both groups to see which can do it more quickly and accurately. If time permits, repeat the game so teams can improve their time.

MATERIALS TO GATHER

Memory verse visual for John 3:17
Backgrounds: Review Chart, Land and Sea, Courtyard, Council Room/Temple
Figures: 1R, R1-R12, 16, 30, 31, 34, 43, 53, 60, 80, 81, 84, 85
Token holders & memory verse tokens for John 3:17
Bible Study Helps for Lesson 12, Part Two
Special:
- *For Introduction:* Word strips WITNESS, MISSIONARY; globe or world map
- *For Bible Content 1 & 2:* "PAUL'S JOURNEYS MAP" poster from Lesson 12, Part One
- *For Summary:* Word strip MISSIONARY
- *For Application:* Newsprint & marker
- *For Response Activity:* "Preparing to Serve God" handouts, pencils
- *For Options:* Materials for any options you choose to use
- *Note: Follow the instructions on page xii to prepare the word strips and the "Preparing to Serve God" handouts (pattern P-8 on page 142).*

🏠 REVIEW CHART

Display the Review Chart with 1R in place. Quickly review lesson themes and verses with the children, placing R1-R12 on the Chart as you progress. Encourage the children to share how they were able to witness to someone recently. Use the following questions to review Lesson 12, Part One:

1. What does it mean to be a witness for Jesus Christ? *(To tell someone what you know about Jesus and how he can save that person from God's punishment for sin)*
2. Who were the first missionaries? *(Paul—or Saul—and Barnabas)*
3. What two things have we learned so far about how a person becomes a missionary? *(A missionary is a person called by God and set apart by a church to witness and help others learn about Jesus.)*
4. What were Paul and Barnabas doing before they became missionaries? *(They were teaching and preaching in the church at Antioch.)*
5. Where did God first send them to witness about Jesus? *(Island of Cyprus)*
6. What happened on the island because they witnessed? *(Many people, including the governor, became Christians; Elymas opposed them.)*
7. Where were the believers first called Christians? *(In Antioch)*
8. What does the word Christian mean? *(Follower of Christ)*

♥ MEMORY VERSE

Use the verse visual to review John 3:17 and its meaning.

📖 BIBLE LESSON OUTLINE

Paul & Barnabas Go to Galatia

▪ Introduction

What is a missionary?

▪ Bible Content

1. Paul and Barnabas travel to Galatia.
2. Paul and Barnabas preach in the synagogue.
3. The Jews reject the gospel; Gentiles believe.
4. Jewish leaders persecute Paul and Barnabas.

▪ Conclusion

Summary

Application
Preparing now to serve God in the future

Response Activity
Being willing to serve God now and in the future

📖 BIBLE LESSON

▪ Introduction

What is a missionary?

(Word strips WITNESS, MISSIONARY; globe or world map)
In our last lesson we learned about two men who witnessed for Jesus *(place WITNESS on the board)*. Who were they? *(Response)* Yes, they were Paul and Barnabas. Who can tell us what a witness is? *(Response)* Yes, a witness is someone who tells what he knows about someone or something. Paul and Barnabas were sent by their church to witness for Jesus in places where the people had never before heard about him.

There is another name for people who do what Paul and Barnabas did. It is "missionary" *(add MISSIONARY)*. Let's say this word together. Does anyone know what a missionary is? *(Response)* A missionary is a Christian who is chosen by God and sent by his church to work full time taking the good news about Jesus Christ to people in other places—either in his own country or in another part of the world *(display globe or map)*. ▲#2

Paul and Barnabas were the first missionaries. They went far from home because they wanted all people to hear the good news about Jesus and be saved. Maybe you, like these men, would like to help

▲ Option #2

1. Print MISSIONARY and WITNESS on flash-cards for children to hold as the words are mentioned.

2. If time permits, have children (as individuals or as a group working on a mural) use markers or crayons to illustrate on newsprint their ideas of what a missionary does. Have them explain their drawings to illustrate missionaries' varied roles in spreading the gospel.

3. Show pictures of missionaries doing different jobs or ministries to expand the children's concept of missionary service.

Note (1)

In this curriculum we have chosen to follow the traditional definition for the word *missionary*. Thus, a missionary is a witness for the Lord Jesus who is...

1. Called by God to serve him vocationally; that is, full time.
2. Sent by a local church, usually under a mission agency, with prayer and financial backing.
3. Involved in activities that relate to evangelism and church planting.

We recognize that there are variations to the traditional definition (e.g. short-term workers, support missionaries and tent-makers), but we believe children need to start with a basic understanding to which those can be added later.

take the gospel to people who have never heard about him. That's how Ross felt as he listened to Mr. Morgan speak at a missionary conference.

Mr. Morgan showed pictures and told about his work as a missionary along the Amazon River in Brazil. He told about the dangers of traveling the river by boat and about the people's strange customs. Finally, he said that there were still many people in the jungle who had never heard that Jesus loves them and died for them. Then he asked everyone to pray that God would send more missionaries to help reach those people.

After the meeting Ross said to Mr. Morgan, "I wish I could go and tell those people about Jesus."

Mr. Morgan was pleased. He said, "Perhaps you can, Ross, when you are older. You can begin preparing right now by learning to be a witness for Jesus at school and in your neighborhood."

That night in bed Ross thought about Chris and Mark and Jason, boys in his class who needed to know about the Lord Jesus. Before he went to sleep, Ross prayed, asking the Lord to help him be a witness to his friends. "And Lord Jesus," he added, "if you want me to, I will be a missionary someday." Then he fell asleep.

Perhaps you, too, have felt you would like to help other people hear about Jesus. Think about it while we hear how Paul and Barnabas—the very first missionaries—went even farther to other parts of the world to witness for Jesus. (1)

Bible Content

1. Paul and Barnabas travel to Galatia. (Acts 13:13,14; Galatians 4:13-16)

Sketch 71   Land & Sea

(Paul 53, Barnabas 80, John Mark 81; "PAUL'S JOURNEYS MAP" poster)

Paul and Barnabas *(place 53, 80 on the board)*, with their helper John Mark *(add 81)*, had seen God do amazing things as they traveled across the island of Cyprus. Knowing that the governor had believed in Jesus must have made them happy and thankful to God. As they boarded a ship to continue their journey, they probably prayed for him and for all the others who had become Christians while they were there. #3

From Cyprus they sailed to Perga *(indicate on the map)*, where John Mark *(remove 81)* left them to return to Jerusalem. The Bible doesn't say why he turned back. Maybe he was afraid of the unknown things ahead or just homesick.

Like everybody else in those days Paul and Barnabas walked as they traveled inland into the Roman province (something like a state) called Galatia *(indicate on the map)*. Today that area is part of the country of Turkey. (2)

It was a very difficult and dangerous trip. They climbed up through steep, rocky mountain gorges where it was very hot and there were often heavy rainstorms which caused sudden flooding. They probably joined a caravan because gangs of thieves would wait along these mountain roads to beat and rob travelers as they passed by. At one point, Paul became very ill. They really had to trust God for help, but they didn't give up. They remembered Jesus' command, "Go into all the world," so they kept on going. God took care of them and kept them safe on this long and dangerous trip.

2. Paul and Barnabas preach in the synagogue. (Acts 13:15-43)

▲ **Option #3**

Distribute markers or crayons and the maps the children marked with Paul's journey route in the last lesson. Encourage them to continue marking his travel route as you show it on the map today. Be sure to collect the maps again after class.

(Crowds 34, 43, 85, Paul 84; "PAUL'S JOURNEYS MAP" poster)

Finally Paul and Barnabas came to a city called Antioch, a different Antioch from the one they had started from *(indicate both cities on the map)*. On the Sabbath day they went to the synagogue where all the Jewish people *(place 34, 43, 85 on the board)* regularly gathered to worship God. There were also some Gentiles there who wanted to know more about God. After the leaders of the synagogue had read from the Old Testament, they asked if their visitors had anything to say to encourage the people.

Sketch 72   Courtyard

Paul *(add 84)* stood and began to speak. He first reminded them of their history as a nation and all that God had done for them when he led them out of Egypt hundreds of years before. Then he talked about the kings God had given them, especially David, and explained how God, through David's family line, had brought the Savior, Jesus, to the Jewish people. He told about Jesus' life, how the rulers of Israel had put Jesus to death, and how God had raised him to life again. Paul showed how this had all been promised to their ancestors long ago, and how God had caused it all to happen, just as their ancient prophets had said he would.

◩ **Note (2)**

This lesson is based on Sir William Ramsey's view that The Epistle to the Galatians was directed to the churches in the Roman province of Galatia (including Pisidian Antioch, Derbe, Lystra and Iconium). Others have held that "Galatians" was an ethnic designation referring to a group farther north, which is never mentioned in Acts.

When Paul had finished, the people said, "Come back next week and teach us more." After the meeting, many people—both Jews and Gentiles—began to talk with Paul and Barnabas about the things they had said. The missionaries encouraged them to believe in Jesus and live like Christians. *(Leave all the figures on the board.)*

3. The Jews reject the gospel; Gentiles believe. (Acts 13:44-49; Galatians 4:12-14)

(Crowd 16, Barnabas 80)

On the next Sabbath day, almost the whole city *(add 16)* came to the synagogue to hear Paul and Barnabas teach *(add 80)*. When the Jewish leaders saw the crowds, they became very jealous and began to argue with Paul.

Sketch 73   Courtyard

Paul and Barnabas spoke boldly: "We came to preach the good news about Jesus to you first. But since you will not accept it, we will go and tell the Gentiles about Jesus and his salvation." When the Gentiles heard that, they were glad and eagerly listened to the Word of God. Many of them believed Paul's message and accepted Jesus as their Savior. Then they went out and told the good news about Jesus to people all over the countryside.

4. Jewish leaders persecute Paul and Barnabas. (Acts 13:50, 51)

Sketch 74   Council Room/Temple

(Jewish leaders 30, 31, men 60, Paul 84, Barnabas 80)
The Jewish leaders *(place 30, 31 on the board)* were not happy to see this happening, so they talked to some of the city's leaders *(add 60)* and turned them against the missionaries *(add 84, 80)*. These leaders then stirred up persecution against Paul and Barnabas. Finally they told them they had to leave the city and never come back.

Paul and Barnabas were probably sad to leave *(remove 84, 80)* these new Christians in Antioch, but they didn't get discouraged and go home. Instead, they went on to other cities in Galatia to witness about Jesus. Because they were obedient to Jesus' command, Paul and Barnabas were able to take the good news about Jesus to places in the world that had never heard of him.

Later Paul wrote a letter to these people in the mountains of Galatia, reminding them of his first visit and thanking them for all their help while he and Barnabas were there. We can read this letter in the New Testament in our Bible. It is called Galatians. ▲#4

▣ Conclusion

Summary

(Word strip MISSIONARY)
Paul and Barnabas were the first missionaries for Jesus Christ who were sent into the world by a group of Christian believers—the church at Antioch.

Who remembers what a missionary is? *(Place MISSIONARY on the board; allow for response throughout.)* Yes, a missionary is a Christian who is chosen by God and sent by his church to work full time taking the good news about Jesus Christ to people in other places. Missionaries are willing to go where God sends them and do the job God asks them to do. That is exactly what Paul and Barnabas did. What happened in each of the places they visited? Yes, many people believed in Jesus as their Savior.

God calls people to be missionaries today, too. First, he wants them to witness for Jesus to people who don't know about him right where they live and work. Then, he calls some of them to serve him in other places

▲ **Option #4**

Have your children find the book of Galatians in their Bibles. Print the words from 4:13-14a on chalkboard or newsprint so the class can read them aloud together. This will help them see how the book of Acts is related to the letters Paul wrote to the people he visited.

in the world. They are like the missionary Ross heard in the beginning of our lesson. Missionaries have to begin preparing long before they go out to serve God full time.

Application

(Newsprint & marker or chalkboard & chalk)
God may choose some of you to serve him as missionaries when you are older. As we learned last week, God wants us to serve him right now by witnessing about Jesus to the people we know. That is one way we can prepare to serve God later as a missionary.

Now let's think about some other ways we can prepare for serving God full time. *(List the children's responses on newsprint or chalkboard. If necessary, suggest the following and add them to the list.)* We can prepare by 1) reading God's Word and praying every day to get to know God better and to hear what he says to us—and someday perhaps even going to college to study the Bible more thoroughly; 2) eating good food and getting proper rest and exercise to keep our bodies healthy; 3) reading about other missionaries in books from the library; 4) doing our best in school; 5) witnessing to others about Jesus; 6) getting to know missionaries and finding out what kinds of things they do to serve God. *(Discuss each point with the class.)* ▲#5

One thing is most important of all—being willing to say to God, "Yes, I am willing to serve you wherever you want me to go, doing whatever you want me to do so that people who have never heard of Jesus or the Bible might come to believe in him."

Response Activity

Invite children who want to say "yes" to God for future service to come talk with you after class. Be careful not to pressure them, but let them know you will pray for them.

Distribute the **"Preparing to Serve God" handouts** *and pencils. Read the handout with the children. Instruct those who are willing to serve God now to check the "YES, I want to begin" box. Instruct those who are willing to do what God wants them to do to check the "YES, I am willing" box. Have them sign their name on the line below and print that day's date on the handout. Encourage them to take their paper home and place it where they will see it every day as a reminder to do what they have promised.*

✍ TAKE HOME ITEMS

Distribute **memory verse tokens for John 3:17** *and* **Bible Study Helps for Lesson 12, Part Two.**

▲ **Option #5**

Before class, print these six points on poster board or newsprint to use as a visual during your discussion.

Or, print the points on individual cards for different children to hold as you discuss each one.

Paul Is Stoned for Preaching
Theme: Faithfulness

Lesson 13

❊ BEFORE YOU BEGIN...

How do we explain faithfulness to today's children? Many of them grow up thinking that if something doesn't please them or seems too difficult, they can just quit and never bother to complete the task. Small wonder! It's not uncommon for persons in our society who don't like a job or an employer or the circumstances in a situation—or a marriage partner—to just quit, seldom considering the consequences for themselves or other people. We need to teach our boys and girls the importance of being faithful to a task, to people and, most importantly, to God—even when it is very hard to do.

Paul and Barnabas proved faithful in extreme and difficult circumstances. God sent them to many cities to witness about Jesus' life, death and resurrection. They were persecuted in each one, but they *never* gave up. They drew on God's power to see them through. Because they were faithful in sharing the gospel, many people who might never otherwise have heard of Jesus Christ came to believe in him as their Savior. *"Moreover it is required in stewards that one be found faithful"* (1 Corinthians 4:2, NKJV).

☞ AIM:

That the children may

- Know that God will help them be faithful witnesses, even in difficult situations.
- Respond by faithfully witnessing to someone who gives them a difficult time.

📖 SCRIPTURE: Acts 14

♥ MEMORY VERSE: John 14:6

I am the way, the truth, and the life; no man cometh unto the Father, but by me. (KJV)

I am the way and the truth and the life. No one comes to the Father except through me. (NIV)

📁 MATERIALS TO GATHER

Memory verse visual for John 14:6
Backgrounds: Review Chart, Plain Background, Courtyard, City Street, City Wall, Plain Interior
Figures: 1R, R1-R13, 5, 6A, 6B, 6C, 6D, 6E, 6F, 6G, 6H, 12, 13, 16, 37, 42, 43, 47, 48, 49, 59, 60, 61, 80, 81, 84, 85, 87, 88, 94
Token holders & memory verse tokens for John 14:6
Bible Study Helps for Lesson 13
Special:
- *For Memory Verse & Bible Content 2b:* Pictures of Greek or Roman gods and/or their temples
- *For Bible Content 1, 2, 3, & 4:* "PAUL'S JOURNEYS MAP" poster from Lesson 12, Part One
- *For Application:* "Trinity" circle (3-part circle only) from Lesson 2
- *For Response Activity:* "Faithfulness" handouts, pencils
- *For Options:* Materials for any option you choose to use
- *Note: Follow the instructions on page xii to prepare the "Faithfulness" handouts, (pattern P-16 on page 146).*

▲ Option #1

Before class, print answers for each review statement on cards, word strips, or paper plates (one item on each).

In class, spread the answers on the floor or a table. As the teacher reads each statement, have a child choose the correct answer and show it to the class. Have the class decide if it is correct.

Or, make two sets of answers and divide the class into two teams. As the teacher reads the review statements, have teams compete to see which can get the correct answer first.

🏠 REVIEW CHART

Display the Review Chart with 1R in place. Choose children to place symbols R1-R12 on the Chart as the class repeats the themes and verses together. Have R13 ready to use when indicated. Have the children complete the statements below to review Lesson 12, Parts One and Two. ▲#1

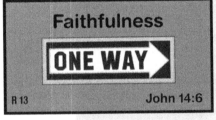

1. A missionary is someone who . . . *(is called by God and set apart by their church to tell people about Jesus and help them live for him.)*
2. Many of the believers left Jerusalem because . . . *(they were being persecuted.)*
3. The church in Jerusalem sent Barnabas to the church at Antioch because . . . *(they had heard the church at Antioch was growing rapidly and they wanted to help them.)*
4. Barnabas brought Saul to Antioch because . . . *(the church was getting so big that Barnabas needed help.)*
5. The governor of Cyprus believed in Jesus because . . . *Paul and Barnabas obeyed God, went to Cyprus as missionaries and taught him the good news about Jesus.)*
6. The Jewish leaders forced Paul and Barnabas to leave the city of Antioch in Galatia because . . . *they were jealous because so many had become Christians.)*
7. Paul wrote the book of Galatians to . . . *(the Christians in the country of Galatia where Paul and Barnabas had preached.)*

Our new building block is called *Faithfulness (add R13 to the Chart)*. What is faithfulness? *(Response)* Faithfulness is being loyal to a choice we make. Those who are faithful are dependable and reliable so other people can count on them to do what they are supposed to do. A faithful friend is your friend all the time, not just sometimes. A faithful worker can be depended on to do what he's supposed to do *all* the time, not just sometimes. Faithfulness is so important that it should be part of our lives.

♥ MEMORY VERSE

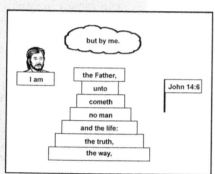

Use pictures of Greek & Roman gods and/or their temples and the verse visual to teach John 14:6.

In Paul's day, the Jewish people worshiped the one true God of the Bible, but most of them refused to believe that Jesus was God's Son and their Savior.

The Gentiles worshiped many different gods *(display the pictures)*. The Greeks and the Romans (people who lived in the part of the world where Paul and Barnabas were preaching) worshiped gods whom they thought were like men and women, only stronger and more beautiful. The Greeks called their greatest god Zeus and built beautiful temples where they worshiped him. Hermes, another of their gods, was supposed to be his servant, a good speaker and a swift runner. Some person made these gods out of wood or stone. No matter how beautiful they were, they could not hear or speak or do anything to help those who worshiped them.

Most of the Gentiles did not know about the one true God or about his Son Jesus Christ. They did not know that Jesus had come to earth and died on the cross to make the only way for them to get to heaven. God loved them and wanted them to know about this one way, so he sent Paul and Barnabas to them as missionaries. Our memory verse tells us this important truth that they preached to the Gentiles. *(Display the memory verse and read it aloud with the class.)*

Jesus said these words to his disciples right before he went to die on the cross. Jesus called himself three things. What is the first one? *(Allow for response throughout.)* Yes, he said that he was the *Way*. He is the *only way* anyone can get to heaven. How do we know he is the *only* way? Yes, Jesus said in the last part of the verse that no man comes to the Father but by him—or believing in him. ▲#2

Who is the Father Jesus talks about? Yes, it is the Father God in heaven, the Creator of the universe, the one who sent Jesus into the world to take the punishment for our sin. Jesus said that there is *no other way* to go to heaven to be with God except by believing in him and what he did for us. Believing in other gods will never get us there. That's why God sent Paul and Barnabas as missionaries to the Gentiles, and why he sends missionaries all over the world today.

What is the second thing Jesus called himself in our verse? That's right; he said he was the *Truth*. That means we can believe what he says

▲ **Option #2**

List on newsprint or chalkboard children's suggestions of ways people think they can get to heaven; for example, going to church, being good, doing kind things.

Discuss why people think these ways are right and why it is difficult for them to come through Jesus.

no matter what other people may say. he always tells us the absolute truth.

What third thing does he call himself? Yes, he is the *Life*. He came to earth to show us who God is and what he's like, and to make it possible for us to have eternal *Life* with him someday in heaven.

Both Jews and Gentiles of Paul's day needed to hear this message. So Paul and Barnabas continued to witness faithfully about Jesus in different countries, even though it sometimes meant they would have difficult times and even be in danger. *(Work on memorizing the verse.)* ▲#3

📖 BIBLE LESSON OUTLINE

Paul Is Stoned for Preaching

▪ Introduction

Andy makes a choice

▪ Bible Content

1. Paul and Barnabas preach the gospel in Iconium.
2. Paul and Barnabas preach the gospel in Lystra.
   a. Paul heals a man who could not walk.
   b. The people try to worship Paul and Barnabas.
   c. The people stone Paul and leave him for dead.
3. Paul and Barnabas return to the cities they had visited.
4. Paul and Barnabas go home to the church in Antioch.

▪ Conclusion

Summary

Application
   Being a faithful witness

Response Activity
   Choosing to witness to someone who gives them a difficult time

📖 BIBLE LESSON

▪ Introduction

Andy makes a choice ▲#4

Andy had to make a choice one day. He had promised to rake the leaves around the house after school. This was very important because his dad had just come home from the hospital and wasn't able to do the job. Andy wanted to help his dad, so he got started as soon as he got home. But it was a bigger job than he had expected, and soon he was tired. Raking leaves wasn't fun anymore.

▲ Option #3

Memorizing the verse: Give the children a minute to study the verse before removing the verse visual and placing the pieces in a basket or paper bag. Allow the children to take turns drawing a piece from the basket or bag and then telling the words on the piece which comes before that one in the verse.

Variation: Have them give the words on the piece which comes after the piece they draw. Time the game or declare it over when all the pieces have been drawn. Place the words back in the basket; have children each draw a piece and place in its proper place in the display as the class says the verse aloud.

▲ Option #4

Have several boys mime the story as the teacher reads it aloud. Then have the class do short skits to act out their choice of a conclusion.

Just then Jack and Fred came by on their bikes. "Hey, Andy," Jack called out, "come on over to Fred's and shoot some baskets with us!"

"Can't yet," Andy answered. "I have to finish the leaves first." But when they were gone, he looked around and thought, "I will *never* get finished in time to shoot baskets tonight!"

What choice did Andy have to make? Which was more important—helping his dad or playing with his friends? Which would be more fun? What would be the faithful thing to do? *(Encourage response.)*

We've been learning how Paul and Barnabas traveled through some dangerous places so they could preach the gospel to people who had never heard it. Today we will see what it meant for them to be faithful as they witnessed for Jesus in some very difficult circumstances.

■ Bible Content

1. Paul and Barnabas preach the Gospel in Iconium. Acts 14:1-7)

("PAUL'S JOURNEYS MAP" poster; man 94, Paul 84, Barnabas 80, crowd 85, leaders 61) ◰(1)

In our last lesson we learned that Paul and Barnabas were thrown out of Antioch. Why did this happen? *(Response)* It happened because they preached about Jesus and the Jews became angry and jealous. What did Paul and Barnabas do then? *(Response)* They didn't give up and go home because they knew God had sent them to preach about Jesus where people had never heard of him. So they continued traveling through Galatia until they came to a place called Iconium *(use 94 to trace their route on the map).* ▲#5

As they usually did, they went to the Jewish synagogue in Iconium *(place 84, 80, 85 on the board)* where they found Jews and a few sincere Gentiles who wanted to learn about the true God worshiping together. That same day Paul and Barnabas began teaching the good news about Jesus. The people were so impressed by their message that a great many—both Jews and Gentiles—believed.

Once again Jews *(add 61)* who refused to believe Paul's message tried to stir up trouble so other people would not hear the Word of God. But Paul and Barnabas stayed there quite a while, speaking boldly for the Lord. To show that he was the living God and their message was true, God gave Paul and Barnabas power to perform miracles.

Soon the people in the city began to take sides; some were for Paul and Barnabas and others, for the Jews who opposed them. Then the troublemakers began plotting how they could mistreat the missionaries and actually kill them by throwing heavy rocks at them. But God allowed Paul and Barnabas to discover the plan, and they were able to leave the city before they were harmed. However, they left behind many people, both Jews and Gentiles, who had believed in Jesus as their Savior.

◰ **Note (1)**

Use sticky tack or a loop of tape to attach figure 94 to the map.

Sketch 75   Courtyard

▲ **Option #5**

Distribute markers or crayons and the maps the children marked with Paul's journey route in the last lesson. Encourage them to continue marking his travel route as you show it on the map today. Be sure to collect the maps again after class.

2. Paul and Barnabas preach the gospel in Lystra.

a. Paul heals a man who could not walk. (Acts 14:8-10)

("PAUL'S JOURNEYS MAP" poster; crowds 16, 61, Paul 84, Barnabas 80, man 42, man 87)

Paul and Barnabas could have become discouraged and gone home, but they didn't. Instead, God helped them to be faithful and they went on to the next city which was Lystra *(indicate on the map)*. There were many people in this area who had never heard of the one true God or Jesus *(place 16, 61 on the board)*. Many of them worshiped the false gods we talked about earlier, even though they were not real and could not hear their prayers or do anything to help them.

Sketch 76 — City Street

One day as Paul and Barnabas *(add 84, 80)* were preaching in the city, a large crowd gathered to hear them. In the crowd was a man *(add 42)* who was sitting on the street. He had never been able to walk. As Paul preached, this man paid close attention. When Paul noticed him and saw that he believed what he was hearing, Paul called out to him, "Stand up!" Immediately the man who couldn't walk jumped to his feet *(remove 42; add 87)* and walked for the first time in his life! God did this miracle through Paul in order to show his power to the people in Lystra. *(Leave all the figures on the board).*

b. The people try to worship Paul and Barnabas. (Acts 14:11-18)

(Pictures of Greek & Roman gods and temples from Memory Verse; people 60, bull 88)

When the crowd of people saw the wonderful thing that had happened, they began to shout in their own language, "The gods *(display pictures)* have become like men and come down to visit us." They called Barnabas Zeus and Paul Hermes because he was the chief speaker. The priest *(add 60, 88)* who led the worship of Zeus in the nearby temple came with bulls and wreaths of flowers because the people wanted to offer sacrifices to Paul and Barnabas.

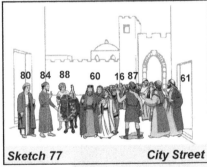

Sketch 77 — City Street

At first Paul and Barnabas couldn't understand what the people were saying. They were probably speaking in their native language which Paul and Barnabas had never learned. When they finally realized what was happening, they rushed into the crowd shouting, "Why are you doing this? We are only men like you! We are not gods! We have come to tell you about the true and living God who made the heaven and earth and the sea and everything in them. Worship him!" But even then, they had a difficult time keeping the people from offering sacrifices to them. *(Remove 60, 87, 88.)*

c. The people stone Paul and leave him for dead. (Acts 14:19, 20)

Sketch 78 — City Street

(Men 47, 48, 49, Paul 59)
Later, some of the Jewish leaders from Antioch and Iconium came to Lystra and began talking to people, turning them against Paul and Barnabas. Soon the very people who were trying earlier to worship them wanted to kill them. They *(add 47, 48, 49)* threw rocks at Paul until they thought he was dead *(remove 84; add 59)*, and then dragged him outside the city and left him there *(remove 59)*.

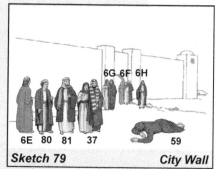

Sketch 79 — City Wall

(Paul 59, 84, people 6E, 6F, 6G, 6H, 37, 81, Barnabas 80) Place 59 on the board.
When the crowd was gone, the believers *(add 6E, 6F, 6G, 6H, 80, 81)* quickly gathered around Paul, grieving because they also thought he was dead. But suddenly he woke up *(remove 59; add 84)*, got to his feet, and walked back into the city with them. He and Barnabas stayed there overnight before traveling on to the next city. It must have been hard to remain faithful at times like that.

3. Paul and Barnabas return to the cities they had visited. (Acts 14:21–25)

("PAUL'S JOURNEYS MAP" poster)
After going on to another city called Derbe *(indicate on the map)* and seeing many come to believe in Jesus there, Paul and Barnabas did an amazing thing! They turned around and went back to all the cities *(retrace their journey on the map)* where they had been mistreated on this trip. Imagine going back to places where people had tried to hurt and even kill you! But Paul and Barnabas were faithful to God and to the job he had asked them to do.

In each city they found a group of people who had trusted Jesus as Savior and were meeting together. The missionaries taught and encouraged the believers to be strong. They also helped the believers in each city to organize a church and to choose leaders to give each church guidance and teaching.

4. Paul and Barnabas go home to the church in Antioch. (Acts 14:26-28)

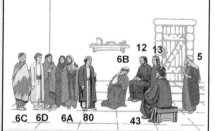

Sketch 80 — Plain Interior

("PAUL'S JOURNEYS MAP" poster; people 5, 6A, 6B, 6C, 6D, 43, 80, Paul 12, Barnabas 13)

As they made their way back down to the seacoast on their way home, Paul and Barnabas continued to preach the good news of Jesus in the towns they passed through. Finally they came to the port city of Attalia *(indicate on the map)*. From there they sailed back to Antioch *(indicate on the map)* and the church that had sent them out as missionaries. They must have been very glad to be home again!

And how glad the church people *(place 5, 6A, 6B, 6C, 6D, 80 on the board)* must have been to see them! They all gathered to hear Paul and Barnabas *(add 12, 13)* tell about their trip. The Bible says the missionaries reported to the people all that God had done through them. Many people, Jews *and* Gentiles, had believed the good news about Jesus. And that there was an organized church in each city now. They praised God together for what he had done in the lives of so many people who had never before heard of Jesus and his love and forgiveness. This all happened because Paul and Barnabas were willing to obey God and serve him as missionaries, faithfully witnessing for Jesus and not giving up when things got difficult.

▪ Conclusion

Summary ▲#6

(Paul 84, Barnabas 80, crowd 16, man 87, people 60, bull 88)

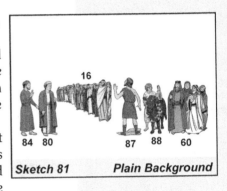

Sketch 81 — Plain Background

What were some of the ways Paul and Barnabas showed faithfulness to God? *(Place 84, 80 on the board; encourage response throughout.)* They didn't give up witnessing even when the Jewish leaders got angry and made them leave some cities or when the people tried to worship them.

What do you think was the most difficult thing that happened to them on this trip? Yes, probably it was Paul's being stoned and left for dead outside of Lystra. What would you have felt like doing then? Yes, we probably would have felt like quitting and going back home where it was safe. But Paul and Barnabas were faithful; they didn't give up, but continued taking the gospel to other cities.

Do you remember what they did before they went back home to Antioch? Yes, they revisited all the cities where they had preached— even those where they had been mistreated, even Lystra where Paul had been stoned! They were faithful! God could count on them to do what he asked them to do.

What had God asked them to do? That's right; he asked them to be witnesses for Jesus to people who had never heard the good news, even when it was very hard to do. According to John 14:6, why did these people need to hear about the Lord Jesus? Correct; Jesus is the only way to the heavenly Father. *Let's say the verse together. (Do so.)*

How were they able to witness in spite of all the hard things that happened to them? Yes, God worked on their behalf and helped them.

What happened because Paul and Barnabas were faithful witnesses for Jesus? Yes, wherever they went many people *(add 16)* believed in Jesus and new churches were formed. A man *(add 87)* who couldn't walk was healed by a miracle of God. Many people *(add 60, 88)* in Lystra stopped worshiping their false gods and turned to the true God. So God allowed them to see the good results of their faithfulness to him even though they had many problems along the way.

Application

("Trinity" circle)

God wants each of us to be faithful, just like Paul and Barnabas were. Their story is an example to show us how God can give us all we need so we can be faithful in doing what he tells us to do.

One important way God wants believers to be faithful is by telling others about Jesus and how he died on the cross and rose again for them. You probably won't have the same kind of problems that Paul and Barnabas did, but it won't always be easy to tell others about Jesus. Some of the kids at school or even your own family may make fun of you or call you names or even get others to stop being friends with you. Does God want you to give up when that happens? No, he wants you to keep on being a faithful witness for Jesus.

How can we have the strength to be a faithful witness when it is difficult to do so? Yes, God the Holy Spirit lives in us *(place "Trinity" circle on the board and indicate the Holy Spirit as you move that section away from the circle)* and is always with us. We can ask him for his help and power any time we need it. He promises to help us.

Will you be faithful in telling others about Jesus? We've been learning that God wants us to be willing to serve him. We've also planned how to witness to someone about Jesus. Were you able to carry out your plan this week? Did you have any problems?   ▲#7

Maybe some of you got discouraged because the person you witnessed to wasn't interested or gave you a hard time. God doesn't want us to be discouraged. He wants us to remember Paul and Barnabas and faithfully follow their example. Don't give up! Keep looking for another opportunity to tell that person about Jesus, just as they did.

Response Activity

Distribute the **"Faithfulness"** *handouts and pencils. Remind the children of the stones that hit Paul because he obeyed God and told people in Lystra about Jesus. Remind the children of how faithful Paul and Barnabas were, even in the very difficult places.*

Ask the children to print their own name on the line under the word faithfulness if they are willing to tell someone about Jesus this week, even

▲ **Option #7**

Ask for volunteers to tell about their experiences in witnessing this week, any problem they faced and what they did about the problem.

if that person makes it very hard for them to do so. Have them take the handout home and put it where they will see it every day as a reminder to obey and be faithful.

As you close in prayer, have the children pray, asking God to help them to be faithful in carrying out their decision. ▲#8

✎ TAKE HOME ITEMS

*Distribute **memory verse tokens for John 14:6** and **Bible Study Helps for Lesson 13**.*

▲ **Option #8**

Before class, collect some flat stones or small flat rocks and use a marker to print the word *faithfulness* on each one. Take the stones and markers to class to use in place of the handouts. Allow any who want to make this commitment to choose a stone and print their name on it; then take it home as a reminder of the promise they have made.

Paul Takes the Gospel to Europe
Theme: Courage

Lesson 14

Part One: Lydia Becomes a Believer

❋ BEFORE YOU BEGIN...

Summoning courage to take a stand for what you believe in a world that lacks absolutes and standards is not easy. And it requires courage to go against the "tide" of a society that has chosen to set its own standards and ridicule those who follow God's truth or any established standard. For children it is especially difficult, because having friends and "belonging" are so important in these growing-up years. For this reason it is also difficult for them to speak of *why* they believe in Jesus Christ and to tell the good news of the gospel in the face of people who might discredit them. As Christians they need to know that a special kind of courage—God's courage and strength—is available to them if God the Holy Spirit lives in them.

Use this inspiring story of the missionaries' willingness to step out into the unknown in obedience to God's command to challenge them to be willing to do the same—to speak up for the Lord and to live for him even when they don't know what the results will be. Show them how God met his servants' needs and how he had already prepared people to hear their message. Encourage them to trust God for the courage they need each day. "Be strong and of good courage; do not be afraid, nor be dismayed, for the LORD your God is with you wherever you go" (Joshua 1:9, NKJV).

☞ AIM:

That the children may

- Know that God gives courage to witness to others and to stand for the truth of the gospel.
- Respond by using the courage God gives them to witness.

📖 SCRIPTURE: Acts 15:1–16:15

♥ MEMORY VERSE: Romans 1:16

For I am not ashamed of the gospel of Christ: for it is the power of God unto salvation to every one that believeth. (KJV)

I am not ashamed of the gospel, because it is the power of God for the salvation of everyone who believes. (NIV)

📁 MATERIALS TO GATHER

Memory verse visual for Romans 1:16
Backgrounds: Review Chart, Plain Background, General Interior, Courtyard, River
Figures: 1R, R1-R14, 6A, 6B, 6C, 6D, 6E, 6G, 14, 17, 24, 30, 31, 34, 43, 44, 60, 80, 84, 85, 89, 94
Token holders & memory verse tokens for Romans 1:16
Bible Study Helps for Lesson 14, Part One
Special:
- *For Bible Content 3:* "PAUL'S JOURNEYS MAP" poster from Lesson 12, Part One; sticky tack or a loop of tape
- *For Response Activity:* "I Will Be a Witness" handouts, pencils
- *For Options:* Materials for any options you choose to use
- *Note:* Follow the instructions on page xii to prepare the "I Will Be a Witness" handouts (pattern P-9 on page 143).

 REVIEW CHART

Display the Review Chart with 1R and R1-R13 in place. Have R14 ready to use when indicated. Review Lessons 9-13 with the following "Who am I" questions:

1. We are God's family here on earth. Who are we? *(the Church)*
2. When I preached on the Day of Pentecost, 3,000 people believed in Jesus as their Savior. Who am I? *(Peter)*
3. I was on my way to the temple to pray when Peter healed a man who could not walk. Who am I? *(John)*
4. We died because we lied about how much money we had given to the church. Who are we? *(Ananias and Sapphira)*
5. I have been called the first Christian martyr. Who am I? *(Stephen)*
6. The Holy Spirit sent me into the desert to tell an Ethiopian man about Jesus. Who am I? *(Philip)*
7. Jesus spoke to me in a bright light while I was on my way to Damascus to persecute the Christians. Who am I? *(Saul)*
8. I came back to life again after Peter prayed. Who am I? *(Dorcas)*
9. Though I worshiped the true God, I did not know about Jesus until God sent Peter to tell me about him. Who am I? *(Cornelius)*
10. I was so surprised to hear Peter's voice that I left him standing at the door after he was miraculously released from prison. Who am I? *(Rhoda)*

What do these people have in common: An astronaut who walks in space, a missionary who goes to live in the jungle and a child who refuses to do wrong with his friends? *(Encourage response; direct answers toward bravery and courage.)*

▲ **Option #1**

Show pictures or models of things which represent power: e.g., trucks, space craft, lightening, results of a windstorm.

▲ **Option #2**

Use the Acts 1:8 visual to review the verse.

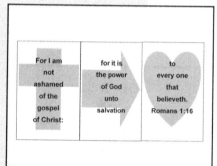

▲ **Option #3**

Refer to the Review Chart and the Salvation symbol (R3). Ask if anyone can say the matching verse (Acts 4:12).

Does having courage mean that you are not afraid? *(Let children respond.)* Does having courage make a job easy? *(More response)* What is courage? *(Response)* Courage is boldness to do what needs to be done even if it seems hard and you are afraid.

Today we complete our model of a Life House. The final building block is *Courage (place R14 on the Chart)*. Courage is a very important part of our Life House, for if we do not have it, we will not tell others the gospel message. The apostle Paul had courage to tell other people about the Lord Jesus—whether at home or in a strange country. He never allowed difficult travel or persecution or illness—or anything else—to stop him. Our new memory verse will help us understand why Paul had such courage.

♥ **MEMORY VERSE**

Use the verse visual to teach Romans 1:16.

Let's read our new memory verse together *(display the verse visual and read it with the class)*. What does Paul say about himself? *(Encourage response throughout.)* Yes, he says he is not ashamed. Ashamed of what? That's right, the gospel of Christ. Why is he not ashamed of the gospel? Because it is the power of God to save people.

When we think of power, we usually think of some thing that is very strong or mighty, like a nuclear bomb or rockets that launch astronauts into space. ▲#1

But God's power is the greatest power of all. We learned about power in another memory verse this year. Who can think of it? *(Response)* Yes, Acts 1:8. Let's say it together: "But ye shall receive power after that the Holy Ghost is come upon you, and ye shall be witnesses unto me." In that verse we learned that God the Holy Spirit living in us would give us power to witness for Jesus. ▲#2

The good news about Jesus' death and resurrection is very powerful. When someone believes it, that person is saved from sin and its punishment. That is called salvation. ▲#3 When Paul believed the gospel message, he was changed from hating Christians to loving the Lord Jesus and his people. That is why Paul could say that he was not ashamed of the gospel. He knew how powerful it is!

Salvation is for everyone who believes the gospel. The power of God to save people from sin and the power of the Holy Spirit living in Paul gave him courage to take the gospel wherever God wanted him to. *(Work on memorizing the verse.)* ▲#4

BIBLE LESSON OUTLINE
Lydia Becomes a Believer

Introduction
Jason has courage to witness

Bible Content
1. Paul and Barnabas go to Jerusalem.
2. Paul revisits the young churches.
3. God sends the missionaries to Europe.
4. Lydia becomes the first believer in Europe.

Conclusion

Summary

Application
Trusting God for courage to witness

Response Activity
Choosing a person and a place where they will witness this week

BIBLE LESSON

Introduction
Jason has courage to witness   ▲#5

Jason had trusted the Lord Jesus as his Savior and wanted to tell his friends about him, but when he tried to tell Randy, Randy just laughed and said that all that "Jesus stuff" was for little kids. Jason felt embarrassed at first. Then he felt hurt because Randy was not interested in Jesus. He thought, "Well, if that's the way he wants to be, I just won't say any more to him!"

What do you think? Should Jason stop witnessing to Randy because he didn't believe in Jesus the first time he heard? *(Let children respond.)*

Jason thought about it some more and then—even though it was hard, he decided to trust Jesus to give him the courage he needed to keep on witnessing to Randy. So he prayed, "Lord Jesus, I know that You love Randy and that You died for him. Help me to trust You for courage to tell him about You again."

Listen carefully to our Bible lesson to see how Paul and his friends showed courage as they continued to travel and tell others about Jesus.

▲ **Option #4**

Memorizing the verse:
Before class: Print verse and reference on a sheet of paper. Make as many copies as you will have teams in your class (2-4). Cut words and reference of each sheet apart; place each set of pieces in an envelope.

In class: Divide group into equal teams and designate one person on each team who can say the verse to be the "verse checker." Line up teams. Have the verse checker with an envelope at the opposite end of the room.

Explain the rules: At the signal, the first person on each team runs to their checker, takes the envelope, empties it on floor or table and puts the pieces in correct order. The checker approves it if correct, mixes up the pieces and puts them back into the envelope while the first child runs back to tag the second person who repeats the action.

The first team to get all its members through the process and then say the verse in unison wins.

▲ **Option #5**

Before class, prepare two boys to act out Jason's story. Encourage them to use their own dialogue.

Bible Content

1. Paul and Barnabas go to Jerusalem. (Acts 15:1-31)

Sketch 82 — General Interior

(Paul 84, Barnabas 80, believers 6B, 14, 17, 43, men 30, 31)

Paul and Barnabas *(place 80, 84 on the board)* must have been glad to be home in Antioch after their long missionary journey. The believers *(add 6B, 14, 17, 43)* were thrilled to hear about all that God had done—how many Gentiles had believed the good news about Jesus and how many churches had been established in different places. ▲#6

One day some Jewish Christians *(add 30, 31)* from Judea (near Jerusalem) came to visit the church in Antioch. They began teaching these Gentile Christians that they had to keep the laws taught by Moses or they could not be saved.

"That's not what we taught the Gentiles on our missionary journey and it's not true!" said Paul and Barnabas. "We are all saved by believing in the Lord Jesus, not by keeping the law!" But the other men kept insisting that Gentile Christians must keep the Jewish laws.

It was important to settle this issue before other missionaries preached to the Gentiles. It must have taken real courage for Paul and Barnabas to stand up for the truth. Finally they and some other men from the church traveled to Jerusalem to talk with the apostles about this serious question.

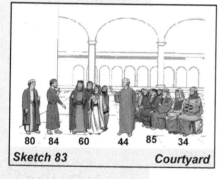

Sketch 83 — Courtyard

(Church leaders 85, 34, 60, Paul 84, Barnabas 80, Peter 44)

Place 85, 34, 60 on the board.

In Jerusalem they *(add 84, 80)* met with the apostles and church leaders. After a long discussion Peter *(add 44)* said, "You know that God called me some time ago to preach the good news about Jesus to the Gentiles so they could believe. (Remember the story of Cornelius?) And God showed that he accepted them by giving them the Holy Spirit, just as he had given him to us. God made no difference between them and us, so how can we say they have to keep laws we couldn't keep? We all are saved the same way—by believing in the Lord Jesus who died and rose again to be our Savior."

Then Paul and Barnabas told about the many Gentiles who had believed and about the miracles and other wonderful things God had done while they were preaching the gospel on their missionary journey.

Finally they all agreed that God had accepted the Gentiles when they believed in the Lord Jesus and received him as Savior and they should do the same. They wrote a letter that Paul and Barnabas took back to Antioch. The Christians there were very glad when they heard this encouraging message. And we can be glad, too, because it means that we don't have to *do* anything to be saved. We just have to believe in the Lord Jesus who died for us and receive him as our Savior.

2. Paul revisits the young churches. (Acts 15:35-16:5)

(Paul 84, Barnabas 80, Silas 6E, Timothy 24, Luke 6C)
After a while Paul and Barnabas *(place 84, 80 on the board)* began thinking about the new believers in all the places they had visited on their missionary journey. Were they all right? Were they still trusting the Lord? Had any more people believed?

Sketch 84 — General Interior

One day Paul said to Barnabas, "Let's go back and see how the believers are doing."

"Yes!" said Barnabas, "I think we should do that. Let's take John Mark with us."

"No," said Paul, "I don't think so. He left us before we were finished with our last trip. We can't depend on him."

"I know," said Barnabas, "but I think he's learned his lesson and we should give him another chance. He will become a good worker if we help him."

But Paul did not agree, and so they decided they would travel separately. Barnabas took John Mark with him and sailed for the island of Cyprus *(remove 80)*. Paul chose Silas *(add 6E)* to be his new partner in revisiting the other churches he and Barnabas had started earlier.

Do you think it took courage for Paul to go back to some of those towns where he had been persecuted? Of course, it did. Where did he get this courage? *(Have children say Romans 1:16 together.)* Knowing that the Holy Spirit lived in him to help him and that the gospel had power to save people gave him courage to go forward and not give up.

Paul was happy to find the churches doing well. Many new believers were worshiping the true and living God through Jesus Christ! The gospel of Christ, the power of God, had truly changed these people when they believed. He stayed a while in each place, encouraging and teaching the people.

In Lystra, Paul was glad to again see a young man named Timothy *(add 24)*. Timothy was probably saved the first time Paul visited Lystra. He had been faithfully serving the Lord and now the men in the church spoke well of him. Paul was very impressed with Timothy and asked him to join him in his work. Along the way they were also joined by Dr. Luke *(add 6C)*, the man who would later write the book of Acts. No doubt, Timothy and Silas were very glad to have a doctor with them to watch over Paul's health and help him in many other ways.

▲ Option #6

Distribute the maps the children marked with Paul's first missionary journey route. Allow them to choose a different color marker or crayon to use as they begin marking the route of his second missionary journey today. Be sure to collect the maps again after class.

3. God sends the missionaries to Europe. (Acts 16:6-12)

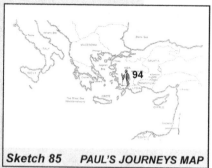

Sketch 85 PAUL'S JOURNEYS MAP

("PAUL'S JOURNEYS MAP" poster, sticky tack or loop of tape; man 94)

After they had visited all the young churches, the missionaries began to consider where they would go next. They decided to go east into Asia *(indicate on the map; attach 94 to the map with sticky tack or loop of tape)* where no one had yet gone to preach the gospel. But the Holy Spirit made it very clear that he didn't want them to go there. Then they thought about going to the north *(indicate on the map)*, but again the Holy Spirit said, "No, that isn't the way." Finally they went to Troas *(indicate on the map)*, a little seaport town, where they waited for God to show them just where they were supposed to go.

In those days before the Bible was completely written down, God often spoke to people in visions—something like a dream. You will remember that Peter saw a vision of a sheet filled with many animals. *(See △(1) on page 65.)* One night Paul had a vision of a man from the country of Macedonia standing and begging him, "Come over to Macedonia and help us." Paul and his companions knew immediately that God had sent this vision and wanted them to take the gospel to Macedonia *(indicate on the map; move figure 94 to each city as you talk about Paul's journey)*.

Macedonia was across the Aegean Sea, a little country north of Greece in Europe. They boarded a ship at Troas and set sail to Neapolis. From there they walked to the city of Philippi. They did not know anyone in that whole region; they had never been in Europe before. But that didn't keep them from going there. They knew God wanted them to go and God gave them courage to make the trip. They trusted that the power of the gospel of Christ would bring many people in this new place to salvation.

4. Lydia becomes the first believer in Europe. (Acts 16:13-15)

Sketch 86 River

(Women 6A, 6G, Lydia 89, Paul 84, men 6D, 6E)

Philippi was a leading city in that whole area, which was ruled by the emperor in Rome. Most of its people worshiped false gods. There were so few Jews living in Philippi that they had no synagogue, so on the Sabbath day they *(place 6A, 6G, 89 on the board)* met by the river to worship and pray.

Paul and his friends spent several days looking around the city and praying that God would lead them to people who were ready to listen to the gospel. On the Sabbath day they *(add 84, 6D, 6E)* went outside the city to the river where they had been told some people gathered to pray. They sat down with the women who were there and told them the good news of Jesus' death and resurrection.

Lydia *(indicate 89)*, a business woman who sold purple cloth, was there that day. The Bible says she was a worshiper of God, and when she heard the good news of salvation through the Lord Jesus, she believed it at once. She became the very first believer in Europe. She gathered all her family and servants together to hear this wonderful message. They also believed when they heard it. Then everyone was baptized to show that they believed in Jesus Christ as the Son of God and wanted to follow him.

After Lydia was baptized, she persuaded Paul and his friends to stay in her home. They went right on preaching the gospel and teaching this new little group of believers. Their courage had been rewarded. They had seen the gospel of Christ, "the power of God unto salvation," at work, changing lives, once more!

Conclusion

Summary

Why did Paul and Barnabas meet with the church leaders in Jerusalem? *(Allow for response throughout.)* Yes, some Jews were teaching that you had to keep the Jewish law to be saved. Why was the meeting so important? That's right; Paul was able to let everyone know what the true gospel message is.

Where has Paul gone up to this point on his second missionary journey? Yes, he went back to the churches he had started in the places where he had been persecuted. Then he continued into Macedonia in Europe. ▲#7

Who was the first person in Europe to believe the gospel and be saved from sin? Correct; it was Lydia.

The power of God to save people from sin when they believe the gospel gave Paul courage to return to the places where he had been persecuted. God also gave him courage to go to some new cities where people heard about Jesus for the first time.

Application

You are not old enough to go on missionary trips as Paul and his friends did, but there are some places where you can witness for the Lord Jesus right now—at school, on the playground, in your home or even at church. Can think of someone in one of those places who needs to hear that Jesus died to save us from sin? *(Response)*

Perhaps you have had an experience like Jason did when he tried to witness to Randy. Feeling afraid to tell someone about the Lord Jesus doesn't mean you don't have courage. You have courage when you tell others about Jesus even though you *are* afraid. You can trust

▲ **Option #7**

Use the "PAUL'S JOURNEYS MAP" poster to review the places he traveled on his second missionary trip.

God to give you this courage. Remember, God has the power to save your friends from sin if they believe the gospel. That is why Paul had the courage to tell it to people he didn't even know. Are you ready to trust God for courage?

Response Activity

Distribute the **"I Will Be a Witness" handouts** and pencils. Have the children circle one of the places listed on their paper and print on the line beside it the name of someone they need courage to witness to. Encourage them to think of how they will witness—giving a tract or invitation to Bible club or telling how Jesus has helped them, etc.

As you close, encourage the children to pray—silently or aloud—telling the Lord that they are going to trust him for courage to be a witness to the one whose name they've written down.

TAKE HOME ITEMS

Distribute **memory verse tokens for Romans 1:16** and **Bible Study Helps for Lesson 14, Part One.**

Paul Takes the Gospel to Europe
Theme: *Courage*

Part Two: The Philippian Jailer Believes

Lesson 14

❋ BEFORE YOU BEGIN...

God's enemy Satan is alive and well on planet earth today, working to keep unbelievers from hearing the Truth and believing it and to distract believers from living as God wants them to. He has duped society into thinking that he and his power are either not real or else something to be played with and enjoyed. People have become desensitized to the danger and evil of his influence through the occult, the media, even toys, music and books. Once he gains children's attention, he quickly "hooks" them.

We must be aware of the forces influencing our children, of the subtle satanic messages they are "buying into." We must faithfully and persistently teach that Satan is God's enemy, but that he is a defeated enemy. That they can say *no* to Satan through the power of the Holy Spirit and have victory over him. And you also must be alert as you prepare and teach this lesson, for Satan hates to be exposed and will try to keep your children from hearing the truth. But our Lord Jesus has won the victory over him at the cross, so we can teach in full assurance of God's power and victory. *"You are of God, little children, and have overcome them, because He who is in you is greater than he who is in the world"* (1 John 4:4, NKJV).

☞ AIM:

That the children may

- Know that God's power can give them courage to resist Satan.
- Respond by trusting God's power to help them resist Satan in their own lives.

📖 SCRIPTURE: Acts 16:16-34

♥ MEMORY VERSE: Romans 1:16

For I am not ashamed of the gospel of Christ: for it is the power of God unto salvation to everyone that believeth. (KJV)

I am not ashamed of the gospel, because it is the power of God for the salvation of everyone who believes. (NIV)

MATERIALS TO GATHER

Memory verse visual for Romans 1:16
Backgrounds: Review Chart, Plain Background, City Street, Prison, Plain Interior
Figures: 1R, R1-R14, 6B, 6D, 6E, 12, 24, 25, 39, 43, 53, 75, 84, 90, 91, 92, 93
Token holders & memory verse tokens for Romans 1:16
Bible Study Helps for Lesson 14, Part Two
Special:
- **For Summary:** Newsprint & marker or chalkboard and chalk
- **For Response Activity:** Newsprint & marker or chalkboard & chalk; "Yes-No" handouts, pencils
- **For Options:** Materials for any options you choose to use
- **Note:** Follow the instructions on page xii to prepare the "Yes-No" handouts (pattern P-18 on page 147).

REVIEW CHART

Display the Review Chart with 1R and R1-R13 in place. Ask a child to name the R14 symbol and place it on the Chart. Review Lesson 14, Part 1 with the following questions:

1. What is courage? *(Boldness to do what's right even if it is difficult and you feel afraid)*
2. Why was it important for Paul and Barnabas to meet with the church leaders in Jerusalem? *(Because some of the Jews were changing the true gospel message.)*
3. Why didn't Paul and Barnabas travel together on a second missionary trip? *(They disagreed about taking John Mark with them.)*
4. Who went with Paul on his second journey? *(Silas, Timothy, Luke)*
5. When did Paul need courage on this journey? *(When returning to the towns where he was persecuted on his first journey and when traveling into Europe)*
6. What gave Paul courage to go to these places? *(He knew the Holy Spirit was in him and the gospel is the power of God to save people from sin if they believe it.)*
7. Who was the first person to believe the gospel in Europe? *(Lydia)*

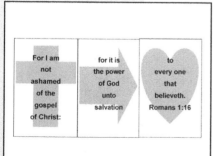

♥ MEMORY VERSE

Review Romans 1:16 by reciting the verse aloud together. Divide the class into three groups. Have each group choose one of the verse parts (as displayed on the visual), then demonstrate it by actions or by acting out what their part means. Encourage a few children to recite the verse by themselves. Finally, recite it all together. ▲#1

📖 BIBLE LESSON OUTLINE

The Philippian Jailer Believes

■ Introduction

Can a psychic help Sarah and Rebecca?

■ Bible Content

1. Paul frees a slave girl from an evil spirit.
2. Paul and Silas are beaten and put in prison.
3. Paul and Silas praise God in prison.
4. God shows his power in an earthquake and a changed life.

■ Conclusion

Summary

Application
Being free from Satan's power

Response Activity
Trusting God's power to resist Satan

📖 BIBLE LESSON

■ Introduction

Can a psychic help Sarah and Rebecca?

Sarah and Rebecca were watching TV when a psychic promised to tell their future if they would call her toll-free number. Sarah thought, "Mom and Dad have been arguing and fighting a lot recently. I wonder if they're going to get a divorce." Aloud she said, "Let's do it!"

"Do what?" asked Rebecca.

"Call that toll-free number," Sarah replied. "Mom and Dad haven't been getting along very well. Maybe the psychic can tell us if they're going to get a divorce."

Another name for a psychic is a fortune-teller. Do you think Sarah and Rebecca should call one? *(Encourage response.)* Why or why not? Where do psychics (fortune-tellers) get their power? That's right; they get their power from Satan. △(1)

Satan is God's enemy and wants people to think that he is more powerful than God. He deceives people through many things, such as fortune-telling, Ouija boards, tarot cards, crystal balls, crystals and horoscopes. Even some Christians have been deceived into thinking

---

▲ Option #1

Provide paper and crayons or markers. Have the children illustrate their ideas of the meaning of the memory verse, either individually or together on a wall mural.

△ Note (1)

Witchcraft, which includes all occult practices such as fortune telling, palm reading and astrology, is strictly forbidden by God in Deuteronomy 18:9-14 because such practices are an affront to him and seen as being in league with Satan.

▲ **Option #2**

Enlarge pattern P-18 and make a large "Yes-No" sign on poster board to illustrate this truth.

▲ **Option #3**

Distribute markers or crayons and the maps the children marked with Paul's journey route in the last lesson. Have them continue marking his travel route as you show it on the map today. At the end of this lesson have the children take their maps home.

Sketch 87 — City Street
(75, 39, 84, 6E, 6D)

that these activities are harmless. But God's Word says to stay away from them.

All people are under Satan's control until they receive Jesus as their Savior. Jesus defeated Satan when he died on the cross and rose from the dead. When we receive Jesus Christ as our very own Savior, Satan's power over us is broken and we are not to have anything more to do with him. The Holy Spirit living in us gives us power to resist (or say no to) Satan when we choose to do what God wants us to do (James 4:7). ▲#2

Satan does not want people to believe the gospel, so he does everything he can to keep them from hearing it. Listen to our story to find out how he did that when Paul and Silas preached the gospel in Philippi, and how God helped them to resist Satan.

■ **Bible Content**

1. **Paul frees a slave girl from an evil spirit. (Acts 16:16-18)** ▲#3

(Paul 84, 53, men 6D, 6E, girl 39, men 75)
One day as Paul *(place 84 on the board)* and his friends *(add 6D, 6E)* were on their way to the place of prayer in Philippi, they met a young slave girl *(add 39)* who was under the control of an evil spirit from Satan. The evil spirit gave her the ability to predict the future. People would pay to have her tell their fortune, so she earned a lot of money for her wicked masters *(add 75)*. Imagine what it was like for her to have an evil spirit living in her body and controlling her mind!

The slave girl began following Paul and his friends, mocking them with the words, "These men are servants of the Most High God, and they have come to show us the way of salvation." The evil spirit wanted to confuse people so they would turn away from the gospel. She kept this up day after day.

Paul became so annoyed that he turned to the girl *(remove 84; add 53)* and spoke to the evil spirit that was in her: "I command you in the name of Jesus Christ to come out of her." Immediately the evil spirit left her, and she stopped shouting for she was now free from Satan's power. That was amazing and all the bystanders knew that it was a wonderful thing. God gave Paul the courage to do this (1 John 4:4).

2. **Paul and Silas are beaten and put in prison. (Acts 16:19-24)** ▲#4

You would think that everyone would be happy for the poor slave girl who was finally rid of the evil spirit. But when the slave girl's wicked masters saw that she could no longer earn money for them by telling fortunes, they were very angry. They grabbed Paul and Silas and dragged them before the city rulers in the marketplace.

"The men are causing trouble!" they shouted. "They are Jews and are trying to get us to keep their Jewish customs. We are Romans and this is a Roman city. We don't want them here!"

(Paul & Silas 90)
A great crowd of people gathered around and joined in the attack. Without giving Paul and Silas opportunity to say a word, the rulers ordered that their coats be ripped off and they be beaten. Then they had them thrown into prison *(place 90 on the board)*. "Don't let them get away!" they ordered the jailer.

The jailer put them in an inner cell in the prison and locked their feet in the stocks. The wooden stocks held their feet so tightly that they could not move their legs, nor could they lie down. Their backs were bleeding, they ached all over and they could only sit up straight with their legs stretched out before them. It was a very uncomfortable and painful position. *(Leave 90 on the board.)*

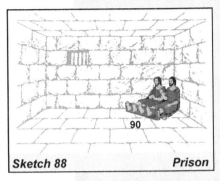

Sketch 88   **Prison**

3. Paul and Silas praise God in prison. (Acts 16:25)

It must have looked as though Satan had won a great victory, but Paul and Silas knew that God was watching over them. They did not give in to discouragement. Thinking about God's power to forgive sin and change people's lives gave them courage to trust God to take care of them and help them through this difficult situation.

Perhaps, as they sat in the dark, dirty prison, they remembered how much the Lord Jesus had suffered for them and they were glad they could suffer for his sake. They did not get angry or begin to complain. Instead, they began to pray and then to sing. The other prisoners heard them singing and wondered how men who had been beaten so badly could sing! How were they able to do this? *(Response)* Yes, the Holy Spirit gave them courage and strength to sing even in this hard place. *(Leave 90 on the board.)*

▲ **Option #4**

Have the children act out Acts 16:19-34 1) as someone reads the passage aloud or 2) to recap the story after the lesson, using their own dialogue for each part.

4. God shows his power in an earthquake and a changed life. (Acts 16:25-34)

(Jailer 6B, arm 91)
At midnight, as Paul and Silas were praying and singing, God did a wonderful thing! A great earthquake shook the foundation of the prison, causing all the doors to fly open and all the prisoners' chains to come loose!

When the jailer—who had been asleep—felt the earthquake and saw all the doors standing open, he thought the prisoners had escaped. If they had, he too would lose his life. He drew his sword, intending to kill himself.

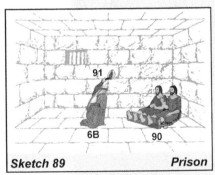

Sketch 89   **Prison**

"Wait!" Paul shouted. "Don't harm yourself! We are all here!"

"All here! How can that be?" the jailer said to himself. He got a light and rushed into the cell where he *(add 6B, 91)* fell down trembling before Paul and Silas. He must have realized that these men had come from God. As he brought them out of the dark prison cell, he asked, "Sirs, what must I do to be saved?"

They answered, "Believe on the Lord Jesus Christ and you will be saved—you and all who live in your house."

Sketch 90   Plain Interior

(Paul 12, man 24, woman 25, Silas 6E, child 92, table 93) Place all the figures on the board.

The jailers' family and servants had all gathered round in the excitement. Now they listened as Paul and Silas told them the good news about Jesus. When they heard how he died and rose again for them, they believed and were saved.

The jailer led Paul and Silas out to where he could wash their sore backs. Afterward the missionaries baptized the jailer and his family to show that they had each believed the gospel and received the Lord Jesus Christ as their Savior. Then the jailer took them into the house and prepared a meal for them. And, the Bible says, the whole family was filled with joy because they had believed in Jesus.

Paul and Silas showed courage by boldly witnessing and preaching—even when they suffered for it—and they saw God's power at work to defeat Satan and to bring the jailer and his family to believe in Jesus. The gospel of Christ "is the power of God unto salvation to everyone who believes." Let's say Romans 1:16 together. *(Do so.)*

▲ **Option #5**

On newsprint or chalkboard, make two columns. Label one Satan's Power; the other, God's Power. List the children's responses under each.

Conclusion

Summary   ▲#5

Sketch 91   Plain Background

(Girl 39, Paul & Silas 90, jailer 24, woman 25)

Let's think back over our story. How did Satan show his power in Philippi? *(Allow for response throughout.)* Yes, he used a slave girl *(place 39 on the board)* to tell people's fortunes and make money for her master, and he used her wicked masters to have Paul and Silas beaten and put in jail so they couldn't preach in Philippi. Was Satan able to keep Paul and Silas from preaching the gospel? No, he couldn't! Why not? That's right; God's power is greater than Satan's.

How did God show his power? Correct, he gave Paul power to command the evil spirit to come out of the girl; he helped Paul and Silas *(add 90)* sing praises to God when they were in jail instead of complaining, becoming discouraged, or getting angry; he sent an earthquake to release Paul and Silas from prison; the Philippian jailer *(add 24, 25)* and those in his household believed in the Lord Jesus.

Application

Jesus won a great victory over Satan when he died on the cross. If you have received Jesus as your Savior from sin, God's Holy Spirit is living in you. He wants to free you from sin's power and help you obey God. He will give you power to resist (or say no to) Satan. You do not need to be afraid of Satan or be controlled by him. God will give you courage to resist Satan. The Holy Spirit living in you is greater than Satan. Whenever you are tempted to sin or be controlled in any way by Satan, you can resist him by saying no to him and yes to God. Tell God that you refuse to do what Satan wants and ask him to help you do what is right. ▲#6

Response Activity

(Newsprint & marker or chalkboard & chalk)

Have the children think of ways Satan has tried to control them or tempt them to sin. List their answers on newsprint or chalkboard. Add anything that you think applies to your group. ▲#7 Have the children read through the list, thinking about what applies to them.

Distribute the **"Yes-No" handouts** and pencils. Instruct the children to print a large NO on one side and under it one way they have been tempted to sin or have allowed Satan to control them.

Remind them that Jesus Christ defeated Satan when he died on the cross and rose again. Have them turn the sign over, draw a large cross in the center and print YES across it.

Encourage your boys and girls to trust God to help them resist Satan any time he tempts them to sin or tries to control them. They can do this by asking God to help them do what is right and declaring that they refuse to do what Satan wants. Give them time to pray silently, telling God that they want to resist Satan and need God's help to do so.

Have them take their hand-outs home and put them where they will see them and be reminded to trust God and say yes to him, and resist Satan by saying no whenever they are tempted to sin.

✍ TAKE HOME ITEMS

Distribute **memory verse tokens for Romans 1:16** and **Bible Study Helps for Lesson 14, Part Two.**

▲ **Option #6**

If you made the "Yes-No" sign, use it here again.

▲ **Option #7**

Give each child who mentions a way Satan tries to control or tempt us the Yes/No sign to hold up:

First the NO side as the class says in unison, "No, I will not _____ (whatever the suggestions was); then the YES side as the class says in unison, YES, I will ask for God's help right now not to _____.

RESOURCE SECTION

Use the materials in this section to help your children
incorporate the Bible truths they are learning
into their daily lives in a practical way.

Transfer the place locations on the Paul's Journeys Map (P-2)
to the felt background map you use when teaching.

Reproduce the patterns as handouts
for the specific lessons where they are recommended.

*Permission granted to reproduce materials in this section
for use with* You Are God's Building *lessons.*

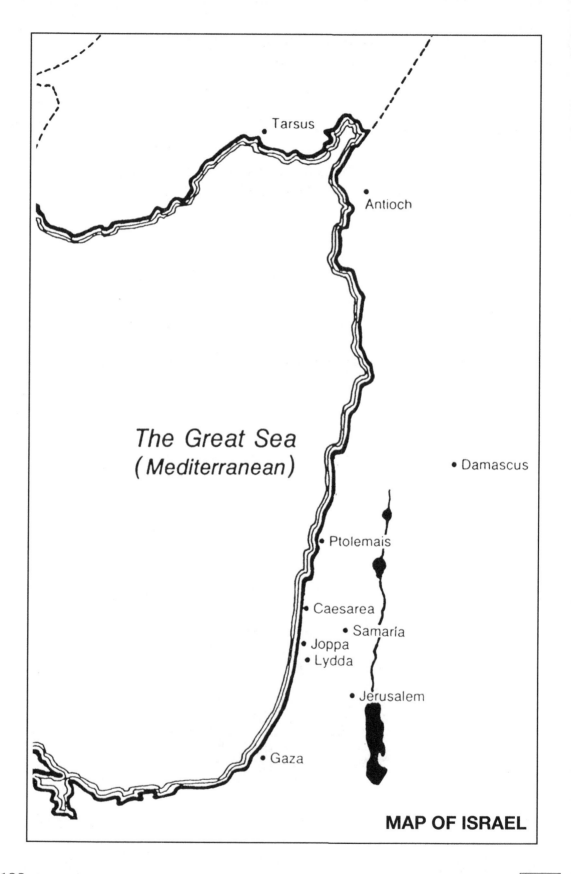

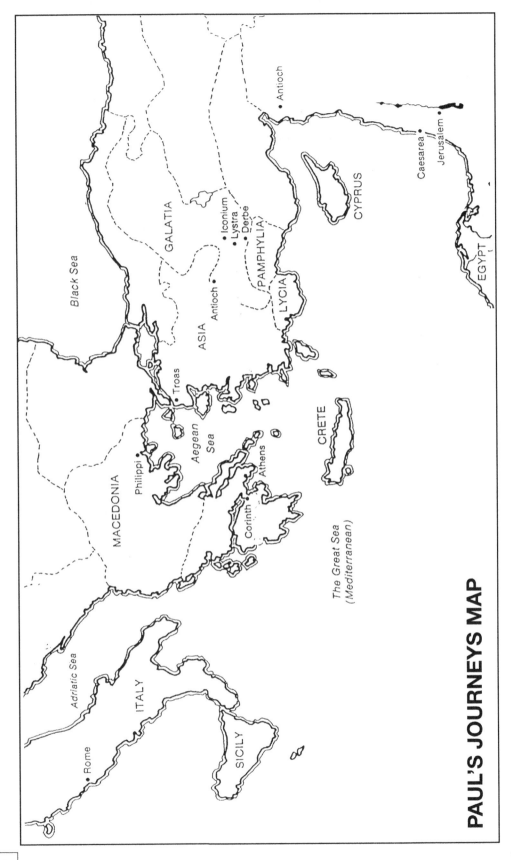

"Jesus and Me"

- ❏ 1. I have already received the Lord Jesus Christ as my Savior and I know I am going to heaven.
- ❏ 2. I'm not sure I understand; I need to learn more about Jesus.
- ❏ 3. I don't know if the Lord Jesus is my Savior.
- ❏ 4. I have never received the Lord Jesus Christ as my Savior.
- ❏ 5. I would like to talk to you about receiving the Lord Jesus Christ as my Savior.

Name _____

P–3

TO TELL THE TRUTH

God wants us to tell the truth.

I was tempted to lie when _____

_____

_____

I chose to give God delight by telling the truth. ❏

P–4

Matthew 5:11

Blessed are you, _____

when someone _____

_____

for my (Jesus') sake.

P–5

God's Word	God Says	I need to obey
John 1:12	Receive Jesus as Savior	_____
Ephesians 6:1	Obey parents	_____
Ephesians 4:32	Be kind, forgive others	_____
Ephesians 4:29a	_____	_____
Exodus 20:15	_____	_____
Proverbs 12:22	_____	_____
Romans 12:13	_____	_____

P–6

A PLAN FOR ACCEPTING OTHERS

*Because God wants all people to hear the gospel and
accepts all who come to him for salvation,
I will show God's love to people who are different from me...*

I will not. . .
- call them names.
- avoid them.
- make fun of them.
- join with others who are mean to them.

I will. . .
- be a friend to them.
- include them in my group of friends.
- get to know them.
- be kind to them.

PRAY for them.

*...so that I may have an opportunity
to tell them about Jesus and what he did for them.*

Signed: _____

P–7

PREPARING TO SERVE GOD

1. Read God's Word and pray every day.
2. Keep healthy by eating good food, getting proper rest and exercising.
3. Do your best in school.
4. Read books about missionaries.
5. Witness to others about Jesus.
6. Meet some missionaries and find out what they do to serve God.

❏ YES, I want to begin preparing to serve God.

❏ YES, I am willing to do what God wants me to do with my life.

Signed _____ Date: _____

P–8

I will be a witness for Jesus...

At school _____

At home _____

On the playground _____

At church _____

**The gospel has power
to save everyone
who believes in Jesus.**

P–9

My Prayer Time

Name _____

1. Praise God.
2. Confess my sins to God.
3. My requests: Answered: Date

   _____   _____

   _____   _____

   _____   _____

   _____   _____

4. Thank God.

P–10

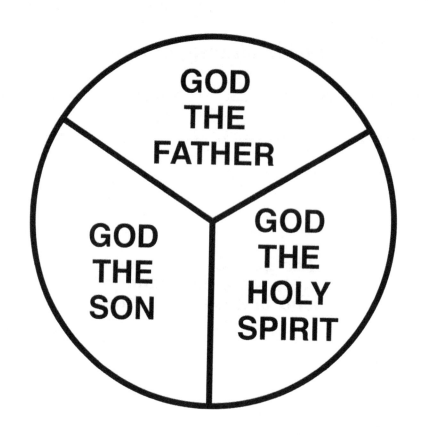

P-11

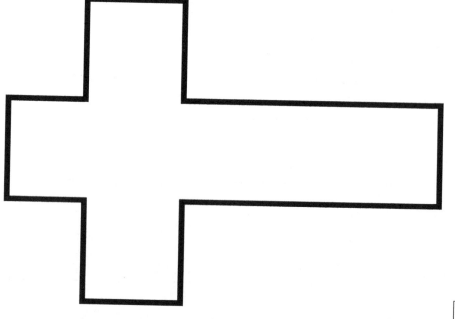

P-12

144

When we receive Jesus as our Savior, he begins to make everything new in our lives.

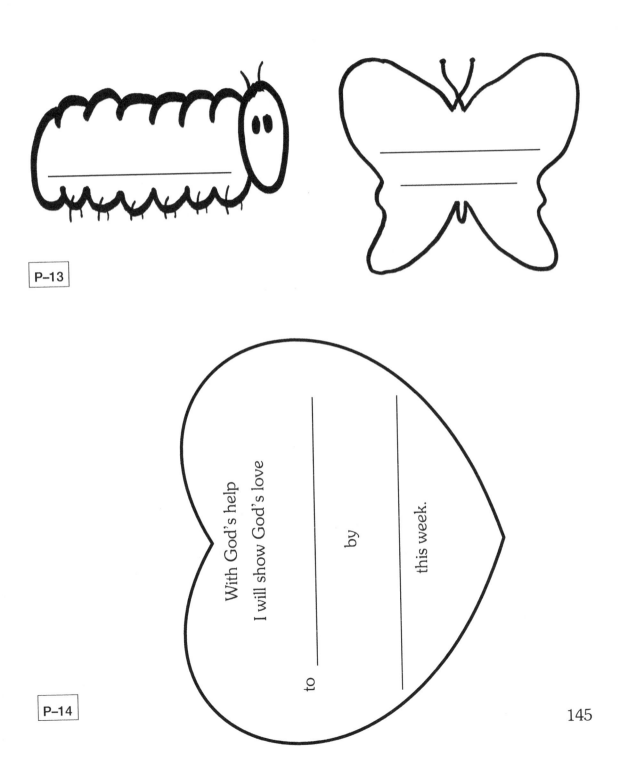

P–15

Faithfulness

_____
NAME

P–16

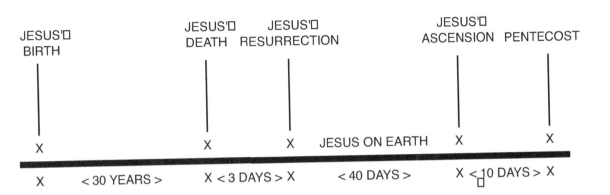

P-17

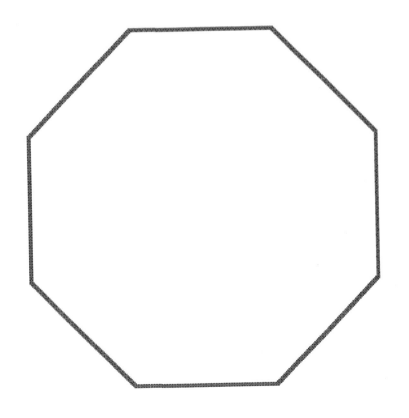

P-18

147

Teaching Materials and Supplies available for

You Are God's Building

Code	Description
FN3T	Teacher's Text

Contains helpful introductory information, 16 unified lessons with correlated visual scenes for felt figures or Powerpoint, sidebar options to enhance interactive learning and notes to expand the teacher's understanding, and a Resource Section with take-home items to visually reinforce student response to God's Word

FN3VCD — Visual CD
  Contains PowerPoint visuals in two tracks (KJV and NIV) for Review Chart, Visualized Memory Verses, and Lessons
  Full-colored flashcards can be downloaded to visualize the lessons.

FN3RCD — Resource CD
  Contains the following:
  Creative Idea Menus
  Visualized Memory Verses (KJV and NIV)
  Student Memory Verse Tokens and Token Holders (KJV and NIV)
  Student Bible Study Helps

FN3TK — Teaching kit with computerized visuals
  Includes Teacher's Text, Visual CD, and Resource CD

FN3F — Felt figures in full color

FN3R — Felt Review Chart

FB — Felt backgrounds in full color
  See the complete list of backgrounds at our ministry store online

FBD — Felt Board
  A 26-inch x 36-inch folding cardboard, covered with blue polyester felt

FBC — Felt Board Clips
  A set of 3 clips to hold felt backgrounds on the Felt Board

TGLM — Tract: *God Loves Me*
  Based on John 3:16; use with children, ages 3-6

TJ316 — Tract: *How to Become a Child of God*
  Based on John 3:16; use with children, ages 7-11

TCG — Tract: *A Child of God*
  Presents salvation and basic teaching for new Christians; use with children, ages 7-11

Order materials online, by phone, or by email

BCM Publications
http://www.bcmintl.org/ministry-store/
Toll-free: 1-888-226-4685
email: publications@bcmintl.org

Mailbox Bible Club correspondence Bible studies
Excellent follow-up material. Contact BCM Publications to order or get a sample lesson.

Made in the USA
Middletown, DE
16 October 2023

40621917R00091